Up *Words*

QUESTIONS JESUS ASKED

KEITH NEWMAN

dustjacket

Published by Dust Jacket Press
UpWords: Questions Jesus Asked / Keith Newman

ISBN: 978-1-953285-69-0

Dust Jacket Press
P. O. Box 721243
Oklahoma City, OK 73172
www.dustjacket.com

 dustjacket

SNU
1899

Dedication

To my wife, Carolyn,
who has a gift for leaving people better than
she finds them, especially me.

◇◇◇

Contents

◆◆◆

Introduction

One of the great joys of my life has been the opportunity to study the New Testament with university students. Though I am the designated teacher, never have I failed to be the student too, who learned more about Jesus and the Holy Spirit inspired words of the New Testament writers. Each semester, my hope and prayer is that these young men and women will fall more in love with the Savior and His Word. I know that in my own life the Bible provides comfort and guidance, new and fresh, every single day.

Since I am responsible for testing their knowledge, I will often remind them in the midst of a class that they might want to make a note because it is coming as a question on a test in the near future. Now teachers have been creating test questions for hundreds of years as a way for students to demonstrate knowledge and celebrate achievement, and while test scores don't measure everything a student has learned; they do provide a marker of their progress along the way.

Jesus was a teacher, and He asked questions. You might even say He gave tests, and they weren't open-book because the Bible would not be printed for another 1400 years. One of the most interesting discoveries for me during my many years of teaching a New Testament Literature and Life course is that Jesus asked His disciples, and others, lots and lots of questions, 307 to be exact. But here is another interesting statistic: Jesus was asked 183 questions. He only answered three.

Scripture is filled with lots of questions and though Hebrew and Greek did not feature punctuation, translators have placed over 3,000 question marks in the Bible. For example, there are 325 questions in the Book of Job and 177 in the Gospel of John. Spend time daily in God's Word and you will have questions; some of those can be answered while others remain with you and can keep you in an ongoing conversation with your Heavenly Father.

Asking questions started early in life for me, and it has never stopped. Some might describe me as *"afflicted with curiosity."* Though I've never thought of it as a malady, I am certain that family and friends might wonder when and if I might cease asking questions. For whatever reason, God wired me up in such a way that I ask more questions than many, and while it has served me well on a number of occasions, I recognize that there are not always answers to the questions I pose. As someone who loves God's Word, I have often found myself pausing, pondering, and praying about the questions I have read. Some of those moments led to the pages that follow.

We learn by asking questions. It starts early in life and never has to end. Mathematician and electrical engineer, Charles Steinmetz, suggests:

"No man really becomes a fool until he stops asking questions."

Inquiry opens doors and more often than not, leads to additional questions. God created us as curious people. Spend a little time with a toddler and hear the confirmation of this truth. "Why?" is one of the first questions we ever ask and our quest for meaning and understanding grows exponentially from those first moments when we are seeking to understand our universe, especially our place and role on this amazing planet.

My love of questions and people who keep asking questions seeking to learn, to grow, and to become better in all of their relationships led me to write these devotionals that are filled with Jesus' questions. Each inquiry comes right out of Scripture. My hope and prayer is that the questions might become words to reflect upon as you walk through your day. God's Word is *"alive and active---sharper than any double-edged sword"* (Hebrews 4:12), and I believe the Spirit will speak as these questions from His Word are pondered and prayed over. As we explore a few of Jesus' inquiries, I hope you will be encouraged and the questions will make you want to know more.

Perhaps you know that Jesus had friends who loved to ask questions. Our Savior operated His own little unaccredited university with students who peppered him with questions. One day, His graduates found themselves staring up into the sky, and I believe they were asking another question:

"What's next?"

Maybe that is a question you find yourself asking as you pick up this book. As you begin each day, you have an opportunity to live out the answer to that question. The good news is that *"we are God's handiwork, created in Christ Jesus to do good works, which God prepared in advance for us to do." (Ephesians 2:10)* May the Spirit use these questions from Jesus to challenge your heart as you seek first the Kingdom of God and live a life of service!

◇◇◇

LOOK UP

*"Look up at the sky and count the stars -
if indeed you can count them."*
Genesis 15:5

Impaired Vision - Matthew 7:3

Excuses - John 5:6

In His Grip - Matthew 14:31

Roadside Assistance - Matthew 20:32

Show Me - Mark 8:12

Beyond Minimum Requirements - Luke 10:26

The Offering Plate - Luke 12:14

Dangerous Curiosity - John 8:43 & 46

Better Witness - John 11:26

Known - John 14:9

◇◇◇

IMPAIRED VISION

*Why do you look at the speck of sawdust
in your brother's eye and pay no
attention to the plank in your own eye?*

Matthew 7:3

I f you've ever visited an optometrist, there is a high probability that you had an experience with a phoropter. These devices feature a number of lenses designed to measure your refractive error and determine your eyeglass prescription. My first encounter with one of these machines was as a 4th grader. I convinced my mom that I was having difficulty seeing. It was a lie. I could see fine. My best friend at the time was a guy named Doug, and he was smart and athletic, and he wore glasses. I wanted to be more like Doug, and I thought glasses would do the trick. So, I tried to fake my way through the eye test with the phoropter. While I was not privy to the conversation between the doctor and my mother, I learned later that it went something like this: *"His eyesight is fine, but there might be something else wrong with him!"*

Jesus addressed the issue of eyesight and lying to ourselves in His Sermon on the Mount. The visual picture He paints is powerful as He compares a speck of sawdust with a plank. Why is it that we so easily see the problems in another person and fail to see our own? One of the painful things I've discovered is that what often seems so obvious to me about another is very similar to what is far too recognizable to others about my life. Ouch!

LOOK UP: Who or what am I currently judging or tempted to judge and what might I be missing in my own life?

The prescription Jesus offers is direct and reminds me of what I often said to my children when they were young. It went something like this: Take care of yourself before you try to make any corrections in others!

The good news is that we do not need an optometrist or a fancy machine to help us find a plank. Some time spent in God's Word, an authentic conversation with a close friend, or more moments of being still can help refine our vision and get us out of the speck inspection business.

Reading for Reflection: Psalms 139:23-24; 2 Corinthians 10:12

*You will never be an inwardly religious and devout individual
unless you pass over in silence the shortcomings of others
and diligently examine your own weaknesses.*
Thomas a Kempis

◇◇◇

EXCUSES

Do you want to get well?

John 5:6

You've probably heard or read the quote about insanity attributed to Albert Einstein: *Insanity is doing the same thing over and over again and expecting different results.* Though there is no evidence that links it to Einstein, the quote has become popular and oft repeated because most of us can identify with it. We've tried something repeatedly with no success, but we are still expecting a breakthrough. Such was the case of the man who had been waiting by the Pool of Bethesda for so many years hoping for a miraculous healing.

Everything changes, it always does, when the man meets Jesus (see John 5:1-15). Jesus asks a simple and somewhat surprising question. Although he has been an invalid for thirty-eight years and his daily presence by the pool, which some believed held miraculous powers, indicated his desire and hope to be healed, Jesus asks him anyway. His answer was not an emphatic, enthusiastic declaration of YES! Instead, he offers an excuse for why he has never been healed. He needs help to get in the pool and others always beat him to the healing moment.

The man, part of a group of invalids, blind, lame, and paralyzed according to Scripture, shared a common belief: their healing was dependent on external circumstances. Before we are too quick to judge, I think it is a common struggle faced by us all. We may find ourselves waiting for the right conditions or support before we take steps toward healing. Yet, Jesus offers a different path – one that begins with the acknowledgment of our need and the desire for change. Jesus' question also highlights the importance of personal agency in our healing process. He doesn't force healing upon the man; instead, He invites him to express his desire to be made whole. This serves as a reminder that we must actively participate in our journey to wellness, whether it be physical, emotional, or spiritual.

LOOK UP: Am I in need of healing in my own life? Do I have a habit that needs to be broken, a relationship that requires healing, or a physical, spiritual, emotional, or financial challenge for which I don't have an answer? Do I want to get well?

Let's be honest, confront our struggles, and seek wholeness in Christ. Let's hear God's voice and respond to His invitation with openness and faith, trusting that He desires to bring restoration to every aspect of our being. In moments of doubt or despair, let us remember that Jesus sees our pain and is ready to heal us. Let us cultivate a heart that longs for His touch, allowing His grace to bring us into a new season of life and hope.

Reading for Reflection: Psalms 103:1-5; James 5:14-16

"Sometimes the miracle you pray for is not the miracle you receive, but the one you give."
Unknown

◇◇◇

IN HIS GRIP

Why do you doubt?

Matthew 14:31

We've heard of "Doubting Thomas," but "Doubting Peter?" As a child I went through a deep period of doubt as the entire male population in my family died or deserted us. At the age of eleven, I was the oldest male in the family and though I had trusted Jesus as my Savior during a summer camp, I doubted. Where was God in the midst of what felt like abandonment? Have you ever been there? Are you feeling that way today?

Simon Peter was impulsive, talkative, wishy-washy, and at times obnoxious, but in Matthew 14, we find him taking a step of faith, out of the safety of the boat and onto water that was cold and wet (see Matthew 14:22-33). Jesus reaches out to Peter as he begins to sink in the waves. Scripture tells us, *"Immediately Jesus reached out his hand and caught him."* One moment there is a demonstration of remarkable faith and in the next instant, fear takes hold, and Peter begins to falter, showing us that even the most faithful can waver in moments of uncertainty.

This story speaks volumes about the nature of faith and the presence of Jesus in our lives. When Peter began to sink, it was not his faith alone that saved him; it was Jesus' immediate response to reach out and catch him. In our moments of doubt and fear, Jesus is always close at hand, ready to lift us up and restore our confidence. We can trust Him.

When we face the storms of life – be it through personal struggles, challenges in our relationships, or uncertainties about the future – we can draw strength from this encounter. Like Peter, we may find ourselves overwhelmed by the waves of circumstances. However, it is in these moments that Jesus invites us to keep our eyes on Him rather than the tumult around us. Jesus offers a gentle rebuke, "*You of little faith,*" which serves as a reminder for us that faith is a journey. It's okay to have doubts; what matters is that we reach out to Him in those moments. When we acknowledge our need for His help, we open the door for His grace to work in our lives.

LOOK UP: Am I acting like a Doubting Thomas or a Doubting Peter? Do I need to look up today and fix my eyes on Jesus, counting on Him to hold me in my moments of fear?

In popular culture, the phrase "Doubting Thomas" describes someone who is skeptical or requires proof before believing something. While the expression can carry a negative connotation, it also serves as a reminder of the human condition – our propensity to doubt and seek assurance in our faith. Remember, Jesus never rebuked Thomas for his doubts, and He will walk alongside you in your uncertainties. As you reflect on Matthew 14:31, remember that no matter how deep the water may seem or how big the worry may feel, Jesus is always there to catch you. Trust in His presence and His power to lift you up. Embrace the journey of faith, knowing that with each step, He is beside you, guiding and supporting you through every step of life.

Reading for Reflection: Psalms 94:16-22; Jude 1:22

Christ never failed to distinguish between doubt
and unbelief. Doubt is can't believe. Unbelief is won't believe.
Doubt is honesty. Unbelief is obstinacy. Doubt is looking
for light. Unbelief is content with darkness.
Henry Drummond

◇◇◇

ROADSIDE ASSISTANCE

What do you want me to do for you?

Matthew 20:32

Should someone restrict me to one devotional book, my decision would not take long. Oswald Chamber's classic, *My Utmost for His Highest*, published after his death, always inspires and challenges me. Born in Scotland, Chambers' early life wasn't marked by exceptional piety. He was a passionate, sometimes rebellious, young man who found his Christian calling later in life. Chambers' ministry was characterized by his intense focus on the practical application of biblical principles to daily life. He wasn't interested in theoretical discussions of theology; he was intensely concerned with how faith should shape our actions and character. He emphasized the importance of absolute surrender to God's will and the necessity of living a life of complete obedience.

Words from Oswald Chambers are a great reminder, and apply so well to the question Jesus posed to the two blind men sitting beside the road (see Matthew 20:29-34).

We calculate and estimate, and say that this and that will happen, and we forget to make room for God to come in as He chooses...Do not look for God to come in any particular way but look for Him. That is the way to make room for Him. Expect Him to come, but do not expect Him in only a certain way. However much we may know of God, the great lesson to learn is that at any minute, He may break in. Always be in a state of expectancy and see that you leave room for God to come in as He likes.

The blind men's plea, *"Have mercy on us, Son of David,"* revealed their faith in Jesus' identity and authority. They acknowledged Him as the Messiah, the Son of David, demonstrating a level of understanding and hope that many around them lacked. Their cry for mercy is not just a simple request for healing; it's an expression of desperation and a heartfelt plea for transformation. It underscores the power of faith to break through barriers and seek help in times of need. Jesus' question, *"What do you want me to do for you?"* is not a dismissive inquiry; it's a thoughtful invitation to articulate their desire and to engage with His power. It challenges us to be clear about our needs and to express them openly to God. Often, we hesitate to ask God for what we need, either due to a lack of faith, feelings of unworthiness, or a fear of being burdensome. Jesus' question encourages us to overcome these hesitations and to approach Him with humility and openness.

The blind men's response, "Lord, let our eyes be opened," is a direct and heartfelt expression of their desire. They are not vague or uncertain about their need; they clearly articulate their longing for healing and transformation. This reminds us of the importance of clearly expressing our needs to God. Vague requests often yield vague answers. Honest and specific prayer allows God to work more fully in our lives.

LOOK UP: How will I articulate a specific need in my life or the life of another today? Will I have the humility and the faith of the blind men to ask God for His help?

Jesus demonstrates His power and compassion in healing these two men. He touched their eyes and restored their sight in response to their stated need. It is in our willingness to express our needs and trust in God's ability to provide that we experience the transformative power of His love. May we be challenged to approach God with clear requests, trusting in His ability to provide for our needs. Let's express our desires with faith and humility, allowing Him to work powerfully in our lives.

Reading for Reflection: Psalms 86:7, John 17:20-23

> *Asking for help is not a sign of weakness.*
> *It is a sign of wisdom and strength.*
> **Unknown**

◇◇◇

SHOW ME

Why does this generation ask for a sign?

Mark 8:12

On more than one occasion I attempted to secure criminal charges against a person that I was convinced had committed a heinous crime only to be told by the prosecutor that I needed to bring more evidence before an indictment could be sought. More often than not, I had great circumstantial evidence, but no, or not enough, direct evidence that a crime had been committed. While frustrated, I understood that the prosecutor had a better understanding and more experience about what was needed to win a conviction in court. The prosecutor wanted someone who had seen the crime committed – a sign.

The question Jesus asks in Mark 8 reveals the tension He faced with the Pharisees, who were seeking evidence of His authority while failing to recognize the miracles He had already performed (see Mark 8:1-13). Jesus' frustration highlights a deeper issue: the hardness of the heart. These religious leaders had been eyewitnesses to countless signs and wonders, yet they remained skeptical. Their desire for a spectacular demonstration was rooted in doubt and disbelief, showing that even when confronted with the miraculous, they could not see the truth before them.

This passage invites us to examine our own hearts. Are there times when we, too, find ourselves seeking signs from God? Perhaps we long for a clear answer or a miraculous intervention in our lives yet fail to recognize the ways God is already at work. Hardness of heart can manifest as doubt, cynicism, or a refusal to see the blessings surrounding us.

Jesus' response reminds us that faith involves trust without always needing signs. It calls us to reflect on our relationship with Him. Do we approach our faith with an open heart, ready to embrace His presence, or do we allow skepticism to cloud our vision? Jesus invites us to look up while we are looking within.

LOOK UP: Am I asking for a sign when I have so much evidence that God has seen me in the past and acted on my behalf? Will I dive into His Word and hear His Spirit calm my doubts?

Let us ask God to soften our hearts and open our eyes. May we seek to recognize His work in the ordinary moments of life and trust in His goodness without demanding miraculous signs. In embracing faith, we find a deeper relationship with Christ, one that flourishes in trust and love. Let us choose to believe in what we cannot see, knowing that God is always present and actively working in our lives.

Reading for Reflection: Job 5:9; Acts 6:8-15

To me, every hour of the day and night is
an unspeakably perfect miracle.
Walt Whitman

◇◇◇

BEYOND MINIMUM REQUIREMENTS

What is written in the law?
How do you read it?

Luke 10:26

What has been your experience with neighbors? Over the years I've heard stories of nightmare neighbors that led to calls for police intervention, lawsuits, and decisions to move away. We have been blessed and though we have lived in multiple states and over a dozen homes, our neighbors have been awesome. Among them are lifelong friends and powerful memories of kindness, compassion, and extra mile service.

The concept of "neighbor" has shifted in meaning across cultures and time periods and is more than a geographical proximity. In Israel, the concept of neighbor was often tied to kinship and tribal affiliation. Neighbors were typically those within one's own clan or community, sharing similar customs, beliefs, and mutual obligations. The emphasis was on reciprocal relationships and shared responsibilities within the group. But, even then, there were examples of extending kindness to strangers, particularly those in need.

Jesus took tests from time to time when someone bold and brash enough would ask Him a question, often in an attempt to trip or trap him. One day an expert in the law inquired about inheriting eternal life and Jesus turned the question around on him and then told a story. The parable, known to many who have never opened a Bible, is called the story of the Good Samaritan (see Luke 10:25-37).

The parable provides a powerful teaching on love, compassion, and the true meaning of "neighbor." The initial question wasn't merely a test of the lawyer's knowledge; it was an invitation to self-reflection. Jesus doesn't provide a simple answer but challenges the lawyer to engage with the Scriptures, prompting him to examine his own understanding and his approach to faith. It's a reminder that true faith is not passive acceptance but active engagement with God's Word. We must not only know the Scriptures but also understand their implications for how we live our lives.

The lawyer correctly quotes the commandments to love God and love your neighbor, but his response reveals a lack of clarity regarding the meaning of "neighbor." The parable of the Good Samaritan is a story that redefined his understanding of who constituted a neighbor and how we should respond to those in need. The parable recounts a traveler who is robbed and left half-dead on the road. A priest and a Levite, figures expected to embody religious piety, pass him by without offering help. However, a Samaritan – a member of a despised group – stops to assist the wounded man, demonstrating extraordinary compassion and selfless service. The Samaritan's actions highlight the importance of empathy and action over religious adherence. Jesus concludes the parable by asking the lawyer, *"Which of these three do you think was a neighbor to the man who fell into the hands of robbers?"* This question forces the lawyer to confront his own biases and preconceived notions. The answer – that the Samaritan, despite societal expectations, was the true neighbor – challenges the lawyer's understanding of compassion and expands his definition of who deserves love and care.

LOOK UP: Do I limit my compassion to those within my own social circles, or am I willing to extend love and service to everyone, regardless of their background or status? What needs to change in my heart and my actions to view everyone I meet as my neighbor?

We are challenged to examine our own hearts. Let's remember that true love transcends differences, whatever they may be, and requires selfless action. Love everyone who crosses your path and create a ripple effect that can change our world.

Reading for Reflection: Leviticus 19:18; Romans 13:8-10

Not everyone is your brother or sister in the faith, but everyone is your neighbor, and you must love your neighbor.
Timothy Keller

◇◇◇

THE OFFERING PLATE

*Man, who appointed me a
judge or an arbiter between you?*

Luke 12:14

One of my memories from adolescence was sitting in a church service next to a young graduate student from the University of Houston. Wayne was studying architecture and we both attended this very small church. Looking back now I am fairly certain Wayne was doing me a great favor by letting me hang out with him. On this particular Sunday night, the offering plate was passed and Wayne put in a quarter and kind of laughed. I simply passed the plate on without contributing. Wayne leaned over to me and said, *"I'm a poor college student, what's your excuse?"* Wayne understood about as well as anybody I have ever known that one of the questions God asks is this: *What are you going to do with what you've been given?* I should tell you one other thing about Wayne that I did not learn until several years later. Wayne, the poor college student, paid my way anonymously to camp the following summer. While I have no idea where Wayne is today, I hope he knows that he made a good investment with what little he had.

An unnamed man in a crowd asks Jesus for help with getting an inheritance from his brother and Jesus chooses to respond with a question (see Luke 12:13-21) and then a story about a rich farmer who focused solely on accumulating possessions, neglecting his spiritual life and ultimately facing a tragic end. The story serves as a cautionary tale about the dangers of materialism and the importance of prioritizing spiritual values over worldly possessions.

The rich farmer in the parable harvests a bountiful crop and plans to expand his barns, believing he has secured his future. He is consumed by his material wealth, seemingly confident in his self-sufficiency. However, God judges his actions, declaring, "You fool! This very night your life will be demanded from you. Then who will get what you have prepared for yourself?" This sudden and unexpected death highlights the fragility of life and the futility of placing our trust in material possessions.

This parable serves as a powerful warning to all of us. It's easy to become preoccupied with accumulating wealth, believing it will bring happiness and security. However, Jesus reminds us that true fulfillment is not found in material possessions but in a relationship with Him. Our focus should be on seeking God's kingdom and His righteousness, trusting that He will provide for our needs.

LOOK UP: Am I living in a way that reflects my faith, or am I primarily focused on accumulating wealth and possessions?

Let's consider how we can live in a way that honors God. May we prioritize our relationship with Him above all earthly pursuits, recognizing that true wealth lies not in what we accumulate but in our devotion to Him. Let's strive to live with a spirit of generosity and stewardship, using our resources to serve others and reflect God's love in the world. May we remember that our lives are temporary, and true fulfillment is only found in seeking God's kingdom and His righteousness. Let's be like Wayne!

Reading for Reflection: Ecclesiastes 3:1-14; Matthew 6:20

Your peers will respect you for your integrity
and character, not your possessions.
David Robinson

◇◇◇

DANGEROUS CURIOSITY

Why is my language not clear to you?
Can any of you prove me guilty of sin? If I am telling the
truth, why don't you believe me?

John 8:43 & 46

M agicians fascinate me. Their ability to use the art of deception in a positive and fun way is captivating. The word "deception" itself holds a fascinating duality. It's a word that describes an action, the act of misleading or tricking, but it also speaks to a state of being, a condition of being misled or misinformed. This inherent contrast makes it a powerful word, capable of evoking a range of emotions and thoughts.

Consider the story of Pandora's Box in Greek mythology. Pandora, tasked with guarding a jar, was explicitly warned not to open it. She failed. Curiosity, a human trait often connected to deception, overwhelmed her. The consequences of her action highlight the devastating power of deception, not only in the act of deceiving but also in succumbing to being deceived. The story isn't just about Pandora's actions; it's about the vulnerability inherent in human nature, our susceptibility to being misled by curiosity or temptation.

Jesus engages in a powerful exchange with the Jewish leaders about the stark choice between truth and deception (see John 8:31-47). He poses two crucial questions, found in verses 43 and 46, which challenge our understanding of faith, identity, and the nature of truth. These questions, though seemingly simple, expose the fundamental conflict between those who are open to truth and those who are bound by deception. Jesus' words are not merely a rebuke of the Jewish leaders but a call for self-examination that resonates with all people across time.

His first question offers a crucial insight into spiritual understanding. Hearing isn't merely about the physical ability to perceive sound; it's about the willingness of the heart to receive and accept truth. The Jewish leaders, blinded by their preconceived notions and self-interest, were unable to truly hear Jesus' message. Their hearts were closed, their minds hardened. This inability to hear stems not from a lack of clarity in Jesus' words but from a spiritual deafness caused by their own resistance to truth.

The second question about belief directly challenged their skepticism. Jesus asserts His truthfulness, highlighting the absurdity of their refusal to believe in the evidence before them. Their disbelief is not based on a lack of evidence but on a willful rejection of truth. They chose to cling to their own interpretations rather than embrace Jesus' message of transformation and redemption. These questions are not just directed at the Jewish leaders of Jesus' time; they are directed at each of us today. We, too, face the choice between truth and deception. We can choose to embrace the truth found in Jesus Christ, allowing His words to shape our lives, or we can cling to our own self-deceptions and rationalizations.

LOOK UP: Do I identify with the world and its values, or do I identify with Christ and His teachings?

The path of truth, though challenging, leads to freedom, joy, and eternal life. The path of deception, however appealing it may seem, ultimately leads to emptiness, despair, and separation from God. Let us not be deceived. Choose wisely.

Reading for Reflection: Genesis 3:1-7; Colossians 2:4

Deceivers are the most dangerous members of society.
They trifle with the best affections of our nature,
and violate the most sacred obligations.
George Crabbe

◇◇◇

BETTER WITNESS

And whoever lives by believing
in me will never die. Do you believe this?

John 11:26

Though death seemed to come often in my family, the first funeral I ever attended was as a young adult. A close friend from high school was home from college when some high school students from his brother's school slashed the tires of their cars parked in the horseshoe driveway. My friend gave chase and was stabbed, dying in the street in front of his home. I attended his funeral, but my only memory is the loud sobbing of the young woman he was dating. My friend was shy, and I had introduced the two of them and helped set up their first date several years prior to his death. Standing in the back of the funeral home chapel, I cried because I was not certain my friend believed in Jesus, and I felt responsible. All these years later, I still feel responsible. I could have been a better witness.

Lazarus, Martha and Mary's brother and friend of Jesus was dead (see John 11:1-44). Scripture does not tell us the cause or story behind his passing, only that he has died. Jesus arrives too late, and offers Martha comfort in her grief but also a powerful declaration of the hope found in Him. Martha, filled with sorrow and confusion, acknowledges her belief in Jesus as the Messiah. Yet, Jesus challenges her to deepen her faith by affirming the promise of eternal life. His question, *"Do you believe this?"* is not just for Martha; it reverberates through time, inviting each of us to examine our own faith in Him.

This Scripture serves as a reminder of the central message of the Gospel: through Christ, we are offered the gift of eternal life. In a world often marked by uncertainty and loss, Jesus' promise stands as a beacon of hope. The assurance that those who believe in Him will never die transcends the physical reality of death, offering a glimpse into the eternal life that awaits us in His presence.

As we reflect on this verse, we are invited to consider our own beliefs. Do we truly grasp the magnitude of what Jesus offers? In moments of doubt, fear, or sorrow, we can cling to this promise. It reminds us that our faith is rooted in the assurance of life beyond this world – a life characterized by peace, joy, and the fullness of God's presence. Jesus' question prompts us to share this hope with others. In a world that often feels hopeless, we are called to testify to the life-transforming power of Christ. Just as Martha's faith was deepened through her encounter with Jesus, may our faith be strengthened as we embrace His promises.

LIGHT UP: Do my friends and family know that I believe in Jesus Christ and He is my Savior?

Let Jesus' promise of eternal life fill your heart with hope and courage. Trust in His words, and let them guide you through life's challenges, knowing that in Him, we find the ultimate assurance of never truly dying. Let your light shine. Be a witness for Him!

Reading for Reflection: Psalms 27:4; John 3:1-18

God is able to take the mess of our past and turn it into a message.
He takes the trials and tests and turns them into a testimony.
Christine Caine

◇◇◇

KNOWN

Don't you know me, Philip,
even after I have been among you
such a long time?

John 14:9

A thank-you dinner began the most significant relationship in my life. I knew almost nothing about the young lady I invited to dinner as an expression of my appreciation when she bailed me out of a jam. We worked the evening shift together on the 3rd floor of 61 Riesner in downtown Houston. Though we were both homicide detectives with the Houston Police Department, she had her partner, and I had mine, and our paths rarely crossed. When I got tied up on an unexpected case, she volunteered and really insisted on typing a 10-page paper that I had due the next day as I was still working on my college degree. The dinner was not a date, but during that evening, I discovered someone who I wanted to get to know better, and the journey continues now 43 years later.

Jesus' question for Philip sounds to me like a frustrated one (see John 14:5-14). It was posed in the context of Jesus reassuring His disciples about His identity and the nature of His relationship with God the Father. It invites us to reflect on the significance of truly knowing Christ and understanding His character. Jesus had been with His disciples for three years, performing miracles, teaching with authority, and demonstrating God's love in action. Yet, Philip's request to see the Father indicates a misunderstanding of who Jesus is. Jesus' response highlights the truth that to know Him is to know the Father. This moment serves as a reminder that familiarity with Jesus does not automatically equate to a deep understanding of His nature and mission.

Getting to know someone, really know them, is a continuing process, and it is true in our relationship with Christ. We have a goal of drawing closer and more familiar with Jesus. Like the Apostle Paul, who first met Him on the Road to Damascus, *"we want to know Him."* We may attend church, read our Bibles, and engage in Christian community, yet still struggle to fully grasp the depth of Jesus' love and the fullness of His grace.

LOOK UP: How well do I know Jesus? Am I investing in the relationship, spending time in His Word, listening for His voice, praying, and persisting with the goal of knowing Him better?

More questions flow from Philip's experience that require more than a casual response. Are we merely acquainted with the stories about Him, or do we have an intimate relationship that shapes our daily lives? Are we embracing the truth of who Jesus is and allowing Him to transform our faith or are we blending into culture and checking in with Jesus when convenient?

These answers impact how we view ourselves, our purpose, and our interactions with others. When we recognize that Jesus reveals the character of God, we can approach Him with confidence, knowing that He understands our struggles and desires to guide us. Let's seek to deepen our understanding of Christ. May we spend intentional time in prayer and Scripture, inviting Him to reveal Himself to us in new and profound ways. In knowing Jesus more intimately, we find the strength and assurance to live out our faith boldly.

Reading for Reflection: Jeremiah 9:23-24; Philippians 3:10

Once you become aware that the main business
that you are here for is to know God, most of life's problems
fall into place of their own accord.
J.I. Packer

◇◇◇

WAKE UP

Wake up, sleeper, rise from the dead,
and Christ will shine on you.
Ephesians 5:14

Nothing to Wear - Matthew 6:28

Farming 101 - Matthew 7:16

Paradoxical - Luke 12:51

On Guard - Matthew 12:29

Absolute Truth - John 8:46

Memory Lapses - Matthew 16:8-11

Choices - Matthew 20:22

People Pleasing - Matthew 23:33

Sleep Deprived - Mark 14:37

◇◇◇

NOTHING TO WEAR

Why do you worry about clothes?

Matthew 6:28

How many times have you said or perhaps heard it said: "I've got nothing to wear." The words are typically voiced with a bit of frustration, and I discovered years ago that it was not helpful to invite my then-teenage daughter into her closet and begin to show her all sorts of options. She was not amused, and I only aggravated the situation.

Clothing is a multi-trillion dollar-a-year industry today, but when Jesus asked this question His audience would probably have owned a limited wardrobe. Even then, though, clothing was a significant part of the culture. Jesus' question remains relevant and invites us to pause and reflect on the beauty and simplicity of God's creation. Jesus uses the example of flowers, which bloom effortlessly, to illustrate a profound truth about worry and provision.

Flowers do not strive or toil; they grow and flourish simply because they are rooted in the soil that nourishes them. This imagery serves as a reminder that God takes care of His creation in ways we may not always recognize. The vibrant colors, intricate designs, and delicate fragrances of flowers are testaments to God's artistry and care. If He pays such attention to the flowers, how much more will He care for us – His beloved children?

In our daily lives, it is easy to become consumed by worries and anxieties, whether about our future, our finances, or our relationships. We often forget that just as God provides for the flowers, He is also actively involved in our lives. He knows our needs and desires to bless us abundantly. Jesus calls us to trust in God's provision, encouraging us to let go of our worries and embrace faith.

WAKE UP: What is my biggest worry today?

Let us seek to cultivate a heart of gratitude and trust. When worries arise, go for a walk. Examine the beauty all around – the flowers, the trees, the skies – and remember that God is in control. He is our Heavenly Father who delights in providing for us, both our physical needs and our spiritual growth. May we find peace knowing that we are cherished by God, who cares deeply for us. Let us strive to live in the present, trusting that just as He adorns the flowers, He will also adorn our lives with His goodness and grace. And today might be a great day to go through your closet and give something away!

Reading for Reflection: Psalms 55:22; Philippians 4:6-7

The best things in life aren't things.
Art Buckwald

◇◇◇

FARMING 101

*Do people pick grapes from
thornbushes, or figs from thistles?*

Matthew 7:16

Though I've never been a farmer, I once lived on a 122-acre farm and enjoyed all of the benefits without any of the labor. The farmer who leased the land rotated his crops, one year corn and the next beans. No doubt that when he planted corn, he expected to harvest corn, and when he planted beans, anything other than beans growing would have caused him to ask lots of questions about what happened. To quote the Apostle Paul, *"We reap what we sow."* True in a field and true in life, yet there seems to be some surprise in society when the consequences of sin and selfishness are the result of what people continue to plant.

In Matthew 7:16, Jesus poses what seems like a dumb question. Certainly, He knew that everyone knew the answer to His question, but this question compels us to consider the source of true goodness and discernment in our lives. Jesus uses this imagery to illustrate a fundamental principle of life and faith: good fruit comes from good trees, and our lives will ultimately reflect the nature of our hearts.

A regular inventory evaluating the sources of our influences and the outcomes of our choices is a healthy practice. Are we seeking wisdom and guidance from places or people who bear good fruit, or are we allowing ourselves to be swayed by voices that lead us away from Christ? In a world filled with distractions and conflicting messages, this question invites us to be discerning about where we invest our time and energy. Jesus' question encourages honest introspection if we will choose to hit the pause button and take the time. What kind of "fruit" are we producing in our own lives? Our actions, attitudes, and relationships should mirror the love and grace of Christ. If we find ourselves producing "thorns" instead of "grapes," it may be time to examine our hearts and realign our priorities with God's will.

In practical terms, this means surrounding ourselves with influences that inspire us to grow in faith and love. It also means engaging in practices that nourish our spiritual lives, such as prayer, studying scripture, and community fellowship. These are the "good trees" which will help us bear good fruit.

WAKE UP: Am I feeding my soul and my soil with God's Word, a community of faith, and time in prayer, or have I stepped away and become distracted with other things, maybe even good things, but not the best things?

Our world is noisy with lots of competing agendas and activities often designed to keep us from resting, reflecting, and acknowledging Christ as our Savior and Lord. Take some time to consider what influences you allow in your life. Are they leading you toward Christ or away from Him? May we strive to be rooted in Him, producing a harvest that glorifies God and blesses those around us.

Reading for Reflection: Psalms 126:5; James 3:18

Sow a thought, and you reap an act; Sow an act,
and you reap a habit; Sow a habit, and you reap a character;
Sow a character, and you reap a destiny."
Charles Reade

◇◇◇

PARADOXICAL

*Do you think I came to bring
peace on earth?*

Luke 12:51

Social media drives me crazy. I love being able to keep up with friends from all around the world. It is great to celebrate their successes and mourn with them in their losses. Having lived in eight different states and made so many connections, the medium available via technology is amazing and also frustrating. While I love the connections, I hate the conflict that so often is exposed when opinions are shared and then, like a tiny spark, a raging fire can begin. So for me, social media is a paradox.

The word "paradox" comes from the Greek word *"paradoxon,"* which literally translates to "contrary to expectation" or "beyond belief." At its core, a paradox is a statement or situation that seems contradictory or absurd but may contain a hidden truth. It challenges our conventional understanding and requires us to look beyond surface-level interpretations to uncover a deeper meaning. Jesus was known for offering a paradox or two, maybe even more.

Such was the case in Luke 12:51, when He declared, *"Do you think I came to bring peace on earth? No, I tell you, but division."* This seemingly paradoxical statement, delivered within the context of His teachings, reveals a profound truth about the nature of truth, faith, and the impact of following Christ. Jesus was not advocating for discord or conflict; rather, He is highlighting the inherent tension that arises when truth confronts falsehood, when righteousness challenges injustice, and when faith confronts doubt.

The arrival of Jesus and His teachings inevitably brought division. His message challenged the religious authorities, who clung to their traditions and power structures. His radical love and acceptance of outcasts and sinners disrupted the established social order. His teachings disrupted long-held beliefs and demanded a radical shift in perspectives. This created conflict and division, illustrating how truth often clashes with the status quo.

Jesus challenges us to consider the implications of living out our faith in a world that often chooses the most popular trend as opposed to the timeless truth of Scripture. Following Jesus may lead to disagreements with friends, family, or colleagues, and not just on social media. Our commitment to His teachings may cause friction with those who hold differing beliefs or values. This is not to say we should seek conflict, but we cannot expect to remain neutral when the truth challenges falsehood.

WAKE UP: Am I willing to embrace the divisive nature of truth? Am I prepared to stand firm in my faith, even when it means facing opposition or criticism?

Jesus' words call us to be courageous and steadfast in our faith. They encourage a willingness to stand up for what is right, even when it is unpopular or difficult. They involve confronting injustice, extending compassion to those who are marginalized, and sharing the Gospel with boldness, regardless of potential conflict. May we strive to live out our beliefs with integrity and courage, remembering that true peace comes not from avoiding conflict but from pursuing righteousness and living according to God's will.

Reading for Reflection: Joshua 1:8-9; John 8:31-32

You and I can discover truth, but we cannot create it. What's true is true and what's not is not – for all of us, all the time. Our culture views truth as something inside us, subject to revision according to our growth and enlightenment. Scripture views truth as something outside us, which we can believe or not but can never sway.
Randy Alcorn

◇◇◇

ON GUARD

*How can anyone enter a strong
man's house and carry off his possessions unless
he first ties up the strong man?*

Matthew 12:29

Count me among those who love rhetorical questions. I've found these questions to be a terrific way to engage an audience, provoke new thoughts, or emphasize a point without seeking an actual answer. Here are a few of my favorites:

- How many times do we have to learn the same lesson?
- Isn't it obvious that we need to change our approach?
- Who among us hasn't faced challenges in life?
- Why not strive for greatness instead of settling for mediocrity?
- What's the worst that could happen if we try?
- Is there anything more powerful than kindness?

Jesus chooses a rhetorical question as He faces off against the Pharisees who always seem to be in an arguing mood, and His question to them is a profound reminder of the spiritual warfare that exists in our lives. The "strong man" represents the forces of evil, and Jesus reveals that before we can overcome these forces, we must first render them powerless.

The image of a strong man bound and incapable of doing any damage speaks to the authority that Jesus has over the darkness in our lives. It encourages us to recognize that we are not powerless in our battles, but rather, we have the ability to confront the challenges we face through the strength given to us by Christ. This verse also emphasizes the importance of preparation and strategy in our spiritual lives. Just as a thief would not raid a well-guarded home without first incapacitating the owner, we must be diligent in our spiritual practices – prayer, scripture study, and community support – to effectively wage war against the adversary.

WAKE UP: Is there a habit or repeated action that is keeping me bound?

As we reflect on this Scripture, let us remember that we are called to be active participants in our faith. We are not merely spectators but warriors equipped with the Holy Spirit. In our daily lives, we can apply this truth by identifying areas where we feel defeated or oppressed and asking God to help us bind those strongholds. With faith and determination, we can reclaim what the enemy has stolen and protect our hearts and minds from further attack.

May we lean on the strength of Christ, who has already won the ultimate victory, and step boldly into the life He has called us to live.

Reading for Reflection: Joshua 1:9; Ephesians 6:10-19

Jesus said nothing about pillows and comfortable retirement.
He launched the invasion of the kingdom of God into a world
held by darkness. He invites you to join him in living in that
startling, dangerous, and beautiful Story.
John Eldredge

◇◇◇

ABSOLUTE TRUTH

*Can any of you prove me
guilty of sin? If I am telling the truth,
why don't you believe me?*

John 8:46

The world wants to tell you that there is no real truth, that you just make it up as you go and all roads lead to heaven, but that is not what the Bible teaches. Twenty-eight times John records Jesus saying, I tell you the truth…" But Jesus came not only to tell the truth but to be the truth. Truth is the plumb line against which all human behavior must be measured, regardless of what society might try to teach.

As someone who has spent over two decades on university campuses, I've experienced the challenge of trying to teach that there is absolute truth in our world. Here's another observation about truth: truth can be believed or denied, accepted or dismissed, obeyed or rejected, celebrated or hated, but no matter what you feel about the truth, it does not change the truth.

Jesus' question captures the tension between truth and unbelief, revealing the heart of His mission and the challenge inherent in accepting His message (see John 8:31-47). The question is not just a challenge to the Pharisees and the religious leaders of His time; it is a question that resonates through the ages. He stands as the embodiment of truth, yet many refuse to recognize Him. This serves as a reminder that the truth can be uncomfortable. It often challenges our preconceptions, confronts our sin, and calls us to change. In a world where opinions are plentiful and truths are often relative, Jesus invites us to engage deeply with the reality of who He is.

The beauty of this passage lies in its invitation to self-examination. When faced with truth, we must ask ourselves: Are we open to recognizing our own shortcomings? Are we willing to embrace the truth of who Jesus is and the implications it has for our lives? It is easy to dismiss uncomfortable truths, but in doing so, we may miss out on the transformative power of Jesus' grace.

WAKE UP: Is there an uncomfortable truth I am avoiding in my own life?

Jesus' unwavering commitment to truth ultimately leads Him to the cross, where He takes the sins of the world upon Himself. This act of love not only demonstrates His innocence but also offers us a path to reconciliation with God. By accepting His truth, we find freedom, healing, and purpose. Could we commit to seeking the truth in our lives and being open to the ways it may challenge us? May we embrace Jesus, the Truth, and allow His words to guide us, transform us, and fill us with hope.

Reading for Reflection: Psalms 111; 2 Timothy 3:16

Your worst days are never so bad that you are beyond the REACH of His grace. Your best days are never so good that you are beyond the NEED of God's grace. Every day should be a day of relating to God on the basis of His grace alone.
Jerry Bridges

◇◇◇

MEMORY LAPSES

*You of little faith, why are you talking among
yourselves about having no bread? Do you still not
understand? Don't you remember the five loaves for
the five thousand, and how many basketfuls you gathered?
Or the seven loaves for the four thousand, and how many
basketfuls you gathered? How is it you don't understand
that I was not talking to you about bread?*

Matthew 16:8-11

Not one, not two, three, or four, but five questions, apparently without a breath! Do you think Jesus in his divinity was experiencing a human moment? The rapid-fire questions remind me of a time or two, maybe more, when my mother took me for a little history lesson as she tried to wake me up and remind me of God's faithfulness in the past and the promises of His Word for the future. Both my attention span and my memory can be less than desired. Anyone else suffer from the same malady?

I take some comfort that despite their eyewitness experience, the disciples struggled with spiritual understanding and faced the danger of forgetting God's past provision. Their focus was on their immediate needs rather than on the power of the One who was with them. Jesus' questions serve as a passionate but gentle rebuke, urging them to remember His previous miracles as evidence of His ability to provide. This moment challenges us to consider our own spiritual awareness.

How often do we, like the disciples, forget the ways God has provided for us in the past? When faced with new challenges or uncertainties, it can be easy to become consumed by worry, losing sight of God's faithfulness. Jesus reminds us that faith should not be rooted in our circumstances but in the character of God, who has proven Himself time and again.

As we reflect on this passage, let us take time to recall the ways God has worked in our lives. Have there been moments when He provided for us in unexpected ways? By remembering these instances, we build a foundation of faith that can sustain us in future trials.

WAKE UP: What am I forgetting about how God has provided for me in the past (make a list), and what issue(s) am I currently facing that requires me to have faith in His provision?

Jesus' words remind us that spiritual understanding requires intentional reflection. We are called to grow in our faith, learning from our experiences and from Scripture. Just as the disciples needed to deepen their understanding, we too, must seek to know Christ more fully and rely on His promises. Let's pray for clarity and faith, and may we be quick to remember God's past faithfulness and slow to doubt His ability to provide in the present. In doing so, we can cultivate a deeper trust in Him, embracing the peace that comes from knowing He is with us every step of the way.

Reading for Reflection: Judges 7:1-15; Philippians 1:21

Remember, tomorrow is promised to no one.
Walter Payton

◇◇◇

CHOICES

Can you drink the cup I am going to drink?

Matthew 20:22

Do you have a favorite cup? Mine is a *Yeti* which means "abominable snowman" in Himalayan, a strange name for a cup, but then this *Yeti* is a strange cup. I don't understand it, but when I put something hot in the cup, it stays hot. When I put something cold in, it stays cold. I don't have to tell it if the liquid is hot or cold. There are no switches or buttons on it to set it for hot or cold, it just knows! I would like to open it up and see what is inside because it seems like magic to me. But *Yetis* are expensive, and I think if I were to do surgery on it, it would be messed up and unable to do its thing of hot and cold.

Jesus responds to the request from the mother of James and John with a question about the "cup" from which He is about to drink (see Matthew 20:20-28). This pivotal moment reveals the cost of discipleship and the nature of true greatness in the Kingdom of God. The "cup" Jesus refers to symbolizes His impending suffering and sacrifice. He is foretelling the trials He will endure, leading to His crucifixion. In asking the disciples if they can drink from this cup, Jesus challenges them – and us – to consider the seriousness of following Him.

It is a reminder that discipleship is not about glory and honor, in fact, it is far from it. Discipleship involves a willingness to embrace suffering and sacrifice for the sake of the Gospel. When James and John confidently proclaim, *"We can,"* they demonstrate a common human tendency to underestimate the challenges of faith. It's easy to desire the blessings that come with following Jesus, but we must also recognize the trials that accompany that journey. Jesus' question serves as a reminder that true discipleship calls for humility, endurance, and a readiness to bear our own crosses.

What was in Jesus' cup? An unbelievably excruciating death by crucifixion; nails driven through His hands and feet; hanging naked at the town garbage dump just outside of Jerusalem. Jesus accepted His cup, and He asks us to do the same. I'm guessing there are some great things in your cup, but also some unwanted challenges, some of your doing, and some that have been thrust upon you. Whatever is in your cup, God will bless and work for good if you present it to Him.

WAKE UP: What is in your cup today and how are you handling it?

Let's follow Him wholeheartedly, even when the path becomes difficult. Jesus invites us to lay down our ambitions and desires and align ourselves with His will. We can embrace the fullness of discipleship, which includes both joys and challenges, and seek to understand the depth of Jesus' sacrifice and respond with a willingness to face our own challenges with courage and faith. Ultimately, true greatness in the Kingdom of God is found in serving others and following Christ's example of love and sacrifice.

Reading for Reflection: Psalms 108:1-7; Romans 8:28

Discipleship is a long obedience in the same direction.
Eugene Peterson

◇◇◇

PEOPLE PLEASING

*How will you escape being
condemned to hell?*

Matthew 23:33

A re you a people pleaser? Do you struggle when anyone is upset with you? Will you bite your tongue to keep from offending someone, even when you disagree with their position? Wanting to be liked, accepted, and even loved is healthy, but seeking human approval at all costs leads us down a road of compromise and defeat. I know, I've done it. Though better today than in years gone by, I confess to being a person who likes to be liked. I've matured, I hope, to the point where I believe being respected as someone seeking God first means much more to me than the approval of others.

Matthew 23 is a chapter that can be difficult to read because Jesus minces no words in addressing the scribes and Pharisees (see Matthew 23:29-36). He gives them a strong, direct, and solemn warning: *"You snakes! You brood of vipers! How will you escape being condemned to hell?"* This powerful indictment comes after Jesus rebukes their hypocrisy and self-righteousness, highlighting the grave consequences of rejecting God's truth and pursuing self-serving agendas. Jesus' words are not blowing off steam or a big-time display of anger; they are a passionate expression of concern and a call for repentance. He recognizes the spiritual danger they are in, the weight of their responsibility, and the severe consequences that would follow their stubborn refusal to embrace the truth. The imagery of *"snakes"* and *"brood of vipers"* gets my attention. These are creatures known for their deceit and venom, and Jesus uses this vivid language to convey the gravity of their actions and the peril of their spiritual state.

The whole chapter is a wake-up call compelling us to consider our own moral responsibility. Are we living in a way that is pleasing to God, or are we allowing our own desires and ambitions to lead us astray? Just as the scribes and Pharisees prioritized their own self-importance over serving God and others, we, too, can fall into the trap of hypocrisy. We may outwardly appear religious while inwardly harboring pride, self-righteousness, or a lack of compassion.

WAKE UP: Is my life bringing glory to God or causing others to stumble? What steps can I take to point people to Jesus and His plan for their life?

Let's examine our hearts and evaluate our actions. Do we truly understand the consequences of our choices? Are we living in a way that reflects the love and grace of God? The question is not merely rhetorical; it underscores the urgency of living a life aligned with God's will. The condemnation Jesus speaks of is not just a future punishment but a present reality for those who reject Him. The weight of their actions, the burden of their hypocrisy, and the consequences of their choices weighed heavily on them – and this same weight can affect us if we ignore our moral responsibility.

Today is a great day to examine our own hearts and pray for the courage to confront our own hypocrisy and the humility to seek forgiveness. May we strive to live lives that reflect God's love and grace, knowing that our choices have eternal consequences.

Reading for Reflection: Esther 8:1-6; Galatians 1:10

If you try to please all, you will please none.
Aesop

◇◇◇

SLEEP DEPRIVED

Are you asleep?

Mark 14:37

Years ago, I worked the night shift, and even when I managed to get a good day's sleep, I felt sleep-deprived. Today, I'm much more of an early bird than a night owl, and I've learned the importance of sleep. We know a good night's sleep supports various bodily functions, including immune system strength, heart health, and metabolic regulation, and chronic sleep deprivation can lead to serious health issues.

While we don't know what kind of accommodations or sleep patterns the disciples experienced, we do get a glimpse into the life of three of them when they take a nap in the Garden of Gethsemane (see Mark 14:32-42). Jesus asked:

Simon, are you asleep? Couldn't you keep watch for one hour?

An embarrassing moment for Simon Peter, James, and John, members of Jesus' inner circle. Jesus is about to be arrested and face the agony of the cross. His question highlights the need for vigilance, especially in times of spiritual warfare and impending trials.

The context of this passage is significant. Jesus, fully aware of the suffering that lies ahead, seeks companionship and support from His closest friends. Instead of standing guard with Him, the disciples fall asleep, missing the opportunity to share His burden. Through this, Jesus offers a critical lesson for us: the importance of staying alert and engaged in our spiritual lives.

Life has a way of stealing our time and we get busy, sometimes doing really good things, and we can find ourselves neglecting the best things, those moments that are most important. Challenges demand vigilance. Distractions, weariness, noise, and even complacency can lead us to spiritual slumber. Much like the disciples, we may find ourselves caught up in the demands of daily life, neglecting our time in God's Word, prayer, reflection, and connecting with God. Jesus' question to these three disciples should serve as a wake-up call for us to remain spiritually aware and active.

Being watchful means being intentional about our relationship with God. It involves setting aside time for prayer, studying Scripture, and being in community with other believers. When we cultivate a watchful spirit, we become more attuned to the Holy Spirit's guidance, better equipped to navigate the challenges of life, and more prepared for the battles we face.

WAKE UP: Am I awake to the spiritual realities around me? Am I ready to support others in times of trial?

May we hear and respond to the call of Jesus for watchfulness, embracing the opportunity to grow deeper in faith and love as we walk alongside Him.

Reading for Reflection: Daniel 6:1-28; Acts 14:21-23

Lay before Him what is in us, not what ought to be in us.
C.S. Lewis

◇◇◇

RISE UP

Then Jesus said to him,
"Get up! Pick up your mat and walk."
John 5:8

Faith Boost - Mark 4:30

A Step in the Right Direction - Mark 5:39

Spiritual Amnesia - John 5:47

Family Ties - Matthew 12:48

Power Outage - Luke 8:45

Sand Script - John 8:10

Letting Go - Matthew 17:17

Anchored - Matthew 21:42

No Thanks! - Luke 24:26

Fishless - John 21:5

◇◇◇

FAITH BOOST

*What shall we say the kingdom
of God is like, or what parable
shall we use to describe it?*

Mark 4:30

One of my all-time favorite gifts sits in close proximity to my desk, a vintage glass jar filled with mustard seeds. There is a faded note inside that reads: *Mustard Seeds – 1929*. The glass jar is interesting as it has raised letters: Horlick's Malted Milk – Racine, WIS – USA – Slough Bucks, England. While eBay suggests the jar might be worth $65-75, for me, it is priceless. A wise and thoughtful parishioner gave it to her young pastor during a time when our congregation had tackled what seemed to be an impossible project, relocating the church facilities to the new highway encircling the City of Houston. Our resources were limited, our flock was modest in size, and the scope of what we were attempting was beyond daunting. The naysayers in our midst were a minority, but there were moments when I was tempted to join them. The pastor's pride was on the line, what if we failed? She dropped the jar of mustard seeds by one day with little commentary. She knew that I knew that Jesus used a mustard seed to illustrate the power of even a little faith, and I think she knew that her pastor needed a big boost to his limited faith.

Jesus asks a thought-provoking question about the Kingdom of God that puts a spotlight on the multifaceted nature of God's kingdom and the limitations of human language in fully capturing its essence (see Mark 4:30-34). He frequently used parables – simple stories that conveyed profound spiritual truths – to explain the Kingdom of God. Jesus used parables to recognize the limitations of human understanding in grasping the complexities of God's reign. The Kingdom of God is not easily defined or confined within a single explanation; it transcends our limited perspectives and challenges our preconceived notions. We need some help to comprehend the wonder of the Kingdom of God.

Mustard seeds, among the tiniest of all seeds, miraculously create a tree with large branches that offer birds a place of shade and rest. Jesus invites us to approach our faith with humility and openness, recognizing that we may never fully understand its depths, but the Kingdom of God is not something we can fully grasp with our intellect alone; it requires faith, trust, and a willingness to embrace the mystery. This question also implies a continuous unfolding of God's kingdom. Just as Jesus used various parables to illustrate different aspects of the Kingdom, its reality continues to reveal itself through our experiences, through Scripture, and through the work of the Holy Spirit in our lives. Our understanding of the Kingdom is not static; it grows and deepens over time as we continue to encounter God's love and grace in our daily lives.

RISE UP: Is my lack of understanding a stumbling block in my faith? Am I investing time in reading, praying, meditating, and studying God's Word to gain further understanding? Do I need to participate in a small group Bible study to go further in my faith?

Let's not be limited by our attempts to define or confine it but embrace the wonder and mystery inherent in God's reign. May we be challenged to live out the principles of God's kingdom – love, justice, mercy, and compassion – in our daily lives, becoming active participants in its unfolding reality. Our understanding will continue to grow as we draw closer to Him. May you find your own mustard seeds like mine that have traveled with me to many places and spaces, serving as a reminder to have faith, keep the faith, pray for faith, and walk by faith.

Reading for Reflection: Numbers 13:26-30; Matthew 17:30

I place no value on anything I have or may possess,
except in relation to the kingdom of God. If anything will
advance the interests of the kingdom, it shall be given away
or kept, only as by giving or keeping it I shall most promote
the glory of Him to whom I owe all my hopes in time or eternity.
David Livingstone

◇◇◇

A STEP IN THE RIGHT DIRECTION

Why all this commotion and wailing?

Mark 5:39

Mom passed away unexpectedly in her sleep. It was the Sunday night following her first chemotherapy treatment administered the previous Thursday. Though I was aware of the tough cancer battle before her, the call I received on the West Coast in the early morning hours surprised and saddened me. Phone conversations had been our only contact in recent months as I was living several thousand miles from my mother. As we celebrated her life of faith and devoted Christian service, we gave thanks that she had not suffered and had passed peacefully while sleeping. Going to bed and waking up in heaven would be my preferred choice, though I do not see anywhere that we get to choose.

In Mark 5:39, Jesus asks what seems like a crazy question amidst the grief and despair surrounding the death of Jairus' daughter: *Why are you weeping?* And then He offers what must have seemed to be an even crazier message: *The child is not dead, but asleep.* This seemingly simple statement, delivered in the context of a profound loss, reveals the power of faith, the nature of death, and the hope offered through Christ.

Jairus, a synagogue ruler, had approached Jesus in desperation, pleading for his daughter's healing (see Mark 5:21-43). His faith had brought him to seek Jesus' help, but the news of her death shattered his hope. The surrounding mourners, steeped in the cultural understanding of death, also responded with grief and despair. Yet, Jesus, seeing beyond the immediate reality, declares that the girl is not dead but asleep. Jesus' statement is more than a gentle reassurance; it's a declaration of His authority over death. He uses the metaphor of sleep to reframe the situation, shifting the focus from the finality of death to the possibility of restoration. It suggests that death, in its ultimate sense, is not the end but a transition and that He holds the power to reverse this transition. This story challenges us to consider our own understanding of death and loss.

RISE UP: Is there something I don't understand today, a request I have made, and heaven is quiet, a relationship that needs hope, or maybe a person in my life that needs healing? Will I trust God's timing and believe that all things work together for good to those who love Him?

In a world marked by sorrow and suffering, we often succumb to despair when faced with the death of a loved one. We may focus on the pain of separation, the permanence of loss, and the uncertainty of the future. Yet, Jesus' words offer us a different perspective – a perspective rooted in hope and faith. May we move beyond our limited understanding of death and embrace the hope that is found in Him. He is the one who holds the keys to life and death, the one who conquers darkness and brings light into our lives. Let's trust in His authority over death, allowing His words to bring peace to our hearts. Just as He awakened Jairus' daughter from death's sleep, He can bring restoration to our lives and offer us the gift of eternal life.

Reading for Reflection: 1 Kings 17:17-24; Romans 6:8

For many of us the great danger is not that we will
renounce our faith. It is that we will become so distracted
and rushed and preoccupied that we will
settle for a mediocre version of it.
John Ortberg

◇◇◇

SPIRITUAL AMNESIA

*But since you do not believe what
he wrote, how are you
going to believe what I say?*

John 5:47

Can you remember the first time you were ever disappointed? Two instances from my childhood stand out in my mind. The first involved cartoons and the other involved cereal. Growing up I was a huge fan of Popeye, and I watched while he tore open cans of spinach with his bare hands and was suddenly transformed into a muscular specimen. Since I wanted to be like Popeye, I asked my mother to buy me some cans of spinach. Big mistake! She insisted on cooking it since I had no ability to open the can with my measly muscles, and after she cooked it, I ate it. I was one disappointed little boy. Disappointed in the taste of spinach, disappointed in Popeye, and disappointed with life. My cereal disappointment came when I saved box tops in order to send away for a Magic Decoder Ring that did 123 different things. When the big day arrived and the ring was delivered in the mail, I discovered it was a piece of junk. Again, I was disappointed!

While those are childish examples, disappointment has a way of showing up from time to time in all of our lives. Someone cataloged these disappointments in a list:

Nothing is as easy as it looks; everything takes longer than you think; if anything can go wrong, it will.

The other line always moves faster.

The chance of the bread falling with the peanut butter and jelly side down is directly in proportion to the cost of the carpet.

Inside every large problem is a series of small problems trying to get out.

When Jesus found his followers struggling to have faith, He reminded them of their forefather, Moses, a leader who had experienced more than his fair share of disappointment (see John 5:45-47). Remember the moment when his followers were thirsty, and apparently, they had forgotten all God had done for them. Spiritual amnesia had set in; something far too common in my own life. But God was patient, and He had a solution for them. Marah was a place of thirst. Elim was a thirst-quenching place, and guess what, it was only five miles away! Twelve springs, seventy palm trees, and lots of water, and Moses and friends would spend the next month there.

RISE UP: How do I get from a place of disappointment to places of delight?

Moses and the Children of Israel made it to Elim from Marah by doing the basics, putting one foot in front of the other. They kept going, kept believing, persevered, and discovered the value of not quitting. Let's put aside our spiritual amnesia and remember that God is always patient and He keeps His promises!

Reading for Reflection: Isaiah 44:1-8; James 1:2-4

> *We must accept finite disappointment,*
> *but never lose infinite hope.*
> **Martin Luther King, Jr.**

◇◇◇

FAMILY TIES

*Who is my mother,
and who are my brothers?*

Matthew 12:48

USA TODAY called Carlos Rogers the most unselfish man in the National Basketball Association. Playing eight seasons on five different teams, Rogers worked long and hard to achieve his dream of playing in the NBA. His path was not easy and the investments he had made to reach this high level of success were significant. Suddenly, the news media was abuzz because he was possibly throwing it all away. Why? Carlos' sister was sick, very sick. She could not survive without a new kidney. Carlos Rogers left his job in the NBA to go home and donate one of his kidneys to his sister. He knew it would end his career . . . but compared to his love for his sister, he didn't care. When I learned of his story I was not surprised at his decision because it was his sister. We love our families, and we make sacrifices, even ones that may not make sense to those looking on. Compare and contrast Carlos Rogers' story with what we read about Jesus' reaction to His mother and brothers who do not need a kidney but just a conversation. (see Matthew 12:46-50)

While Jesus is teaching, his mother and brothers show up outside the door seeking a few minutes of His time. Jesus appeared to dismiss the presence of his biological family and highlight the importance of His spiritual family. This story challenges our traditional understanding of family and underscores the importance of spiritual kinship. This spiritual family transcends blood ties, extending to all those who embrace His message and strive to live according to His will. The message is simple: our commitment to Christ should supersede all other earthly allegiances. This is not a dismissal of family but a re-ordering of priorities, placing our relationship with God and our commitment to His teachings above all else.

We are invited to consider the nature of our own spiritual families. Just as Jesus formed a close bond with His disciples, we, too, are called to cultivate meaningful relationships with fellow believers. It is in these bonds of spiritual kinship that we find support, encouragement, and strength in our faith journeys. This spiritual family transcends geographical boundaries and cultural differences, uniting us in our shared commitment to Christ.

RISE UP: Do I have a community of faith that holds me accountable, encourages my spiritual growth, celebrates with me in moments of victory, and mourns with me in times of loss? Am I providing help and hope to a group of believers on their spiritual journey? Who needs an investment of my time, maybe because they have a limited biological family for support?

We need each other. Let's reflect on the significance of spiritual kinship. Maybe make a list of people who have been your spiritual moms and dads, brothers and sisters. May we be challenged to prioritize our relationships with fellow believers, support one another, and strive together to live out the teachings of Christ. Let's recognize that our true family – the family of faith – is united not by blood but by our shared commitment to follow Jesus and do the will of the Father. This spiritual family offers lasting connections and bonds that transcend earthly limitations. Give thanks for the bond that draws us all together, the love of Jesus. We are all equals at the foot of the cross.

Reading for Reflection: Psalms 122:6-9; Ephesians 2:19-22

We have exchanged love of family and home for
cyberfriends and living in constant motion that robs the
soul from memories – and perhaps from that still,
small voice that longs to be heard.
Billy Graham

◇◇◇

POWER OUTAGE

Who touched me?

Luke 8:45

A gifted Children's Pastor assigned me two of the youngsters in her flock, one was my daughter and the other was the daughter of a member of our pastoral staff. Our assignment was to visit a large local independent living complex where we would go door to door with a wagon to collect donated canned goods for a food drive. The two little preschoolers in my care were dressed in costumes and having a great time, not a care in the world which was easy to do at their age. As we exited an elevator, we came upon a group of seasoned citizens - seated in rocking chairs enjoying each other's company. One of the ladies made a request that had me nervous. She wondered if my daughter would give her a hug. Honestly, I wasn't sure how she might react. These were strangers, harmless and sweet, but you never quite know how a four-year-old might respond. With no prompting from me, my little girl walked over and gave her a hug, and soon others wanted a hug and the next thing I knew, we had a hug fest going on! It was a powerful moment and reminded me of the significance and need for human touch.

You know this story, a woman with a chronic illness reaches out and touches the hem of Jesus' garment, believing that even a small touch would heal her (see Luke 8:40-48). Jesus asks a question that surprises the disciples and is both profound and revealing. The crowd around Jesus is dense, yet He feels a distinct touch – one that comes from genuine faith. This woman had suffered for twelve long years, enduring physical pain and social isolation, prevented from experiencing human touch. Her faith pushed her to reach out to Jesus, believing that maybe, just maybe, His power could change her life.

Jesus stops everything and calls her out of the crowd, not to embarrass, but to demonstrate how much He values personal faith. She took a big risk and demonstrated a tiny bit of faith, and He rewarded her with healing. Like this unnamed woman, Jesus invites us to engage with Him personally, to bring our needs and burdens before Him.

RISE UP: Do I have a need that is incredibly private, maybe known by few, perhaps by no one but me, and would I be willing to reach out, rise up in faith asking Jesus to do a miracle for me?

The woman's touch may have been an act of complete desperation and "Hail Mary" hope, but we, too, are invited to approach Jesus with our struggles, trusting in His ability to heal and restore. We can cultivate a heart that seeks Jesus earnestly. We can reach out to Him in faith, knowing He responds to our cries for help. In every moment of doubt or despair, remember that Jesus is present, ready to bring healing and transformation to our lives. Let us not just be part of the crowd; let us touch the hem of His garment and experience His power in our lives.

Reading for Reflection: Psalms 62:1-8; 1 Peter 2:24

Life is either a daring adventure or nothing at all.
Helen Keller

◇◇◇

SAND SCRIPT

Woman, where are they?
Has no one condemned you?

John 8:10

Embarrassing moments, we've all got them and sometimes it's fun to recall how we dug ourselves out of a difficult situation or the lessons we learned and have vowed never to repeat again. I've got a long list that includes everything from missing a plane because I was reading a book to asking a person if they had been sick because I thought their voice sounded funny. Turns out that was their normal voice! Talk about an awkward moment. Whatever your most embarrassing moment might be, it pales in comparison to the conversation Jesus has with a woman during the Feast of Tabernacles (see John 8:1-11).

The woman, caught in the act of adultery (Scripture provides no details), finds herself in front of Jesus and a group of men, teachers of the Law and Pharisees. We never hear anything about her partner, as she is the sole individual accused of this sin. Their intentions had little to do with seeking justice, but the design was to trap Jesus into making a statement that could be used against Him. According to the Law of Moses, adultery was punishable by stoning (Leviticus 20:10), and they sought to see if Jesus would uphold the law or show mercy – potentially putting Him at odds with the Roman authorities who prohibited capital punishment.

Jesus' response to the accusers is striking. Rather than directly arguing with them, He bent down and wrote on the ground, an action that has spurred much speculation regarding its significance. We have no idea what He wrote in the dirt. When Jesus was pressed for an answer, He responded, *"Let any one of you who is without sin be the first to throw a stone at her."* This statement shifts the focus from the woman's sin to the moral integrity of her accusers. One by one, they leave, convicted by their own consciences.

In these moments Jesus offered compassion over condemnation. He exemplified grace over mercy, choosing not to condemn the woman, but acknowledging the truth of what she had done. Jesus' final words to the woman are not only forgiving but also directive – He calls her to a new life, emphasizing that while grace is freely given, it comes with the expectation of change. We are reminded that God's desire is to restore rather than punish. As for the accusers, Jesus challenges them to consider their own sinfulness, illustrating the importance of self-examination before the judgment of others.

RISE UP: Have I been too quick to judge someone in my circle of influence? What does a self-inventory look like as I consider my own need for grace and mercy from Jesus?

An embarrassing moment leaves us with feelings of awkwardness, discomfort, or self-consciousness, while a shameful moment can create deep regret, guilt, or worthlessness. Jesus wants us to give Him our shame and live as a beloved child of God. As He forgave the woman in John 8, He will forgive all who come to Him and confess our sins. Scripture makes this promise over and over again. May we live in the power of His resurrection and the hope of restoration.

Reading for Reflection: Psalms 51; 1 John 5:9

Repentance is not what we do in order to earn forgiveness;
it is what we do because we have been forgiven.
Brennan Manning

◇◇◇

LETTING GO

How long shall I stay with you?
How long shall I put up with you?

Matthew 17:17

At its core, frustration arises from a perceived gap between our expectations and the reality of a situation. This gap can be minor, like waiting in a long line, or significant, such as facing a major setback in a long-term goal. The intensity of the frustration often correlates with the size of the perceived gap and the importance we place on the desired outcome. We all get frustrated, right? But did Jesus ever get frustrated? It certainly appears to me that He did, and today's questions seem to illustrate the human emotion experienced by the Word who became flesh and moved into our neighborhood.

Jesus responds to his disciples when they ask a simple, but important question: *"Why couldn't we drive it out?"* The disciples had failed in their attempt to heal a demon-possessed boy (see Matthew 17:14-16). Jesus' words, though seemingly directed at their lack of success, reveal a deeper truth about the power of prayer and the importance of persistent faith. The disciples, despite witnessing Jesus' power and authority, struggled to cast out the demons themselves.

We need faith and prayer and God's power to overcome whatever spiritual obstacles confront us. Jesus explained to His disciples that this kind of demon can only be driven out through prayer and fasting. Prayer and fasting are not merely rituals but disciplines that cultivate spiritual dependence on God. Prayer involves humbly seeking God's guidance and strength while fasting represents a conscious setting aside of our own desires to focus solely on Him. Combined, they demonstrate a deep commitment to seeking God's will and relying on His power. This story invites us to reflect on our own prayer lives and ask ourselves some tough questions.

RISE UP: Do I approach prayer with earnest faith, or am I merely going through the motions? Am I persistent in my requests, or do I give up easily when I don't immediately see results?

Jesus' words challenge us to deepen our understanding of prayer, recognizing its power to overcome spiritual obstacles and bring about transformation in our lives. The disciples' failure to cast out the demon was not a sign of their inadequacy but an opportunity for them to learn about the importance of relying on God's power. Similarly, when we encounter difficulties or struggles in our lives, it can be an opportunity to grow in our faith and deepen our dependence on Him.

May we emulate the disciples' desire to heal yet also learn the necessity of prayer and fasting. Through prayer, fasting, and persistent faith, we can experience the powerful work of the Holy Spirit in our lives.

Reading for Reflection: Isaiah 58:6; Matthew 6:16-18

> *Prayer is reaching out after the unseen; fasting is letting go of all that is seen and temporal. Fasting helps express, deepen, confirm the resolution that we are ready to sacrifice anything, even ourselves to attain what we seek for the kingdom of God.*
> **Andrew Murray**

◇◇◇

ANCHORED

Have you never read in the Scriptures:
The stone the builders rejected has
become the cornerstone; the Lord has done this,
and it is marvelous in our eyes?

Matthew 21:42

These days cornerstones are primarily for ceremony as opposed to structure. The date of construction, names of individuals involved in the project, and perhaps the name of the building engraved in the cornerstone provide a historical record and a method of honoring key contributors. Over the years I've been involved in a number of conversations about the names to be included in the limited space of a cornerstone and who might be offended if their name was left out.

Historically cornerstones were important elements in ancient architecture and construction practices. The cornerstone was traditionally the first stone laid during the construction of a building, serving as a reference point for the rest of the structure. Its placement ensures that the building is aligned correctly and is a symbol of stability and strength.

Jesus used the cornerstone metaphor to confront the religious leaders who had rejected Him. He referenced Psalms 118:22-23, illustrating an important truth about His identity and mission. By identifying Himself as the cornerstone, a bold move, Jesus emphasized that He was and is essential to our faith and lives. The builders, representing the religious authorities, rejected Him, failing to see the significance of His presence and teachings. Yet, God, in His sovereignty, has elevated Jesus to the position of the cornerstone, the very foundation upon which our faith is built.

Embracing Jesus as our cornerstone means recognizing His authority in our lives and allowing Him to guide our decisions and actions. It calls us to trust in His plans, even when they challenge our comfort or expectations. When we build our lives on the firm foundation of Christ, we find stability, purpose, and peace.

RISE UP: Are there areas of my life where I have rejected or ignored the teachings of Jesus? Have I chosen to accept the messages that are more convenient and less conflicting with my personal preferences?

When we overlook His guidance, seeking to build our lives on unstable foundations – such as material success, social approval, or even our own understanding, we risk building a life that lacks true purpose and stability. Let us consider how we can better align our lives with Christ as our cornerstone. May we open our hearts to His teachings, allowing Him to shape us and guide us. In doing so, we participate in the marvelous work that God is doing in our lives and the world around us.

Reading for Reflection: Psalms 118:22-29; Ephesians 2:19-22

Any structure must have a strong foundation.
The cornerstones anchor the foundation. For some reason
the cornerstones that I chose to begin with I never changed.
John Wooden

◇◇◇

NO THANKS!

*Did not the Messiah have to suffer
these things and then enter his glory?*

Luke 24:26

Imagine a sign-up sheet in your local church foyer or on the refrigerator at work: Wanted – No Experience Required – Willing to Suffer. Who in their right mind would sign up for suffering? Flip on one of the 24-hour news stations and you won't have to watch long before you hear or see people somewhere in the world experiencing unimaginable suffering. Fires, floods, earthquakes, plane crashes, military coups, the list goes on, but there is a common denominator: people suffering for reasons they did not create and cannot control.

On La Gonave off the coast of Haiti, I led a group of university students who had raised the funds to serve on a construction team for a new hospital, the only one on the island of 100,000 residents. During our time working on this project, the construction superintendent told me a story of one of his workers who had arrived at the work site that morning asking for the day off but was desperate not to lose his job. The conversation revealed some tragic news as my new friend learned that two of the daughters of his laborer had passed away from cholera during the night. He needed the day off to bury his girls but could not afford to lose his job. Suffering had a human face in those moments.

In His post-resurrection appearance, Jesus asked the two men on the road to Emmaus a question for which they had no answer (see Luke 24:13-35). A history lesson began as Jesus started with Moses and the prophets and reminded them of all the Messianic prophecies. He explained the necessity of His suffering as part of God's divine plan. This hard truth invites us to reflect on the relationship between suffering and glory in our own lives.

Suffering was essential for the fulfillment of Scripture and the inauguration of His kingdom. The disciples had hoped for a triumphant Messiah, one who would deliver them from earthly oppression. Yet, Jesus reveals that true glory comes on the other side of suffering. This principle is critical for us to understand as followers of Christ. In our own journeys, we often encounter hardships and trials that can feel overwhelming. Like the disciples, we may question why suffering is part of our experience. However, in moments of pain, we are reminded that God is at work, shaping us and preparing us for greater purposes. Just as Jesus' suffering led to His exaltation, our struggles can lead to growth, deeper faith, and a closer relationship with God.

RISE UP: What suffering am I experiencing or witnessing that leaves me anxious, doubting, and asking the question: Where is God? Can I give it to Him and rise up in the hope that He is awake, aware and that His purpose will ultimately be done?

Let's embrace our challenges and the world's challenges with hope. When we face difficulties, we can trust that God is using them for our good and His glory. Our suffering is not in vain; it can be a catalyst for transformation, both in ourselves and in the lives of those around us. Christ's path to glory involved suffering, and so may ours. May we find strength in our trials, knowing that they are part of a greater, still being written, story.

Reading for Reflection: Psalms 34:18; Romans 5:3-5

A season of suffering is a small assignment when
compared to the reward. Rather than begrudge your problem,
explore it. Ponder it. And most of all, use it.
Use it to the glory of God.
Max Lucado

◇◇◇

FISHLESS

Friends, haven't you any fish?

John 21:5

Though I've never fished for a living, I have spent hundreds of hours on a boat in pursuit of fish. At least some of those experiences have failed to produce even one bite. Frustrating? Yes! Confusing? Absolutely! I knew there were fish in the lake or the ocean, plenty of them, but what I didn't understand was why I couldn't catch at least one. I've talked to the fish, prayed to God, asked my fishing companions for help, and waited and wondered why I couldn't catch a fish. What I never ever appreciated was someone coming along the bank or passing by in a boat and asking me the question Jesus asked of at least a few of his disciples.

After a long, fishless night, (see John 21:1-6) they respond to His question (that He already knows the answer to) with a simple "No." The moment provides a picture of our human experience – efforts that seem in vain and the longing for purpose and provision. The disciples had returned to their old way of life after the resurrection of Jesus, perhaps feeling lost or uncertain about their future. They were skilled fishermen, yet they struggled to catch even a single fish. This scenario mirrors our lives when we find ourselves in seasons of doubt and frustration, working hard but seeing little to no results. It is easy to become disheartened, feeling like our efforts are futile.

Jesus' inquiry invites us to reflect on the deeper significance of our struggles. He doesn't chastise them for their lack of success; instead, He engages them with a simple question that prompts a reassessment of their situation. Often, in our moments of despair, we may overlook the presence of Jesus and the potential for His provision. When we acknowledge our deficiencies and turn to Him, we open ourselves to His guidance. Following Jesus' direction, the disciples cast their nets on the other side of the boat, resulting in an overwhelming catch. This story demonstrates the transformative power of obedience and faith. In our own lives, we might feel the weight of our unfulfilled ambitions or the sting of disappointment. Yet, when we invite Jesus into our struggles, we find that He can turn our "no" into abundance.

RISE UP: Where do I need God's help, and am I willing to ask specifically in faith, confident that He hears my prayers and will respond in His time and in His way?

Consider the areas where you feel stuck or unproductive. Make a list. Be willing to ask for help from God, but perhaps also from others who He may direct you to. Asking for help often causes us to humble ourselves, and admit that we are not nearly as self-sufficient as we would like to be. Listen closely to Jesus' voice and trust in His guidance. Remember, He is ever-present, ready to lead us to the fruits of His labor when we lean on Him.

Reading for Reflection: 2 Chronicles 25:5-8; Hebrews 4:16

The Christian life is not a constant high.
I have my moments of deep discouragement.
I have to go to God in prayer with tears in my eyes, and say,
'O God, forgive me,' or 'Help me.'
Billy Graham

◇◇◇

LIGHT UP

*His lightning lights up the world;
the earth sees and trembles.*

Psalms 97:4

Surprise and Delight - Matthew 5:46-47

Darkness Always Loses - Mark 4:21

Trust and Obey - John 2:4

Conversation Starters - John 4:7

Seen - Mark 5:9

Rapid Fire - Mark 8:17-18

I Know You - Mark 8:27, 29

Anchor Deep - Luke 8:25

Shining Bright - John 11:9

Naughty or Nice - Mark 9:33

◇◇◇

SURPRISE AND DELIGHT

*If you love those who love you,
what reward will you get? Are not even
the tax collectors doing that? And if
you greet only your own people, what are
you doing more than others? Do not
even pagans do that?*

Matthew 5:46-47

My friend loves to practice what she calls: *Surprise and Delight*; the idea is to try and make someone's day, boost their spirit, provide an unexpected lift by doing something special that sends a simple message: *I thought of you, I care, you are important.* With her encouragement and sometimes ideas, I've been able to promote and participate in some of these moments. A card, text, even a small gift, not much time or expense is required to surprise and delight. Here is what I've discovered, it never fails, I always am more blessed than the chosen recipient.

Sitting on the side of a mountain, Jesus challenged his listeners to rise above the ordinary standards of love and kindness. He pointed out, with a string of questions, that loving those who loved them was something everyone did – even those considered the most despised in their society, like tax collectors.

Jesus called the mountainside congregation, and us, to go beyond the ordinary, to do something extraordinary, and it is easier than you may think. The extra-mile love and service was His consistent message throughout the Sermon on the Mount. Jesus knew that extending love to friends and family is easy, but He asks us to love those who may not love us back. This radical love can take many forms: a kind word to a stranger, assistance to a neighbor in need, or even forgiveness to someone who has wronged us. The challenge lies in breaking free from our comfort zones and societal norms. Jesus' words challenge us to redefine our understanding of love. By loving beyond the expected, we not only reflect Christ's character but also impact the world around us. Let us strive to cultivate a love that is radical, inclusive, and transformative.

LIGHT UP: How can we embody a love that is truly transformative and reflective of Christ? Who could I surprise and delight?

Today, try to connect with someone outside your usual social circle. This could be a co-worker you don't know well or a neighbor you've never spoken to. A simple greeting or conversation starting questions can open the door to deeper relationships. Maybe you can look for an opportunity to show kindness to those who may seem unapproachable or different from you. Take a moment to evaluate your relationships. Are there people you avoid or dismiss? Pray for the strength to reach out and show love, even when it's uncomfortable.

Reading for Reflection: Psalms 107:8; 1 Corinthians 13:1-13

He said "Love...as I have loved you."
We cannot love too much.
Amy Carmichael

◇◇◇

DARKNESS ALWAYS LOSES

Do you bring in a lamp to put it
under a bowl or a bed?
Instead, don't you put it on its stand?

Mark 4:21

Years ago, I spent quite a bit of money on batteries. You see, it was an occupational need. I worked the night shift as a police officer, and a powerful flashlight was a tool of my trade. Searching a building where a silent alarm had been triggered, approaching an automobile on a traffic stop, or even trying to find the correct house numbers to respond to a call for help made it a necessity, not an added benefit. Light always pierces the darkness, one hundred percent of the time, and I could not afford to take a chance of having a dead battery.

Jesus posed a question in the context of His teaching in parables, emphasizing the purpose of revelation and the importance of sharing the light of truth. The imagery of a lamp was significant. In Jesus' time, a lamp was essential for illuminating dark spaces, and its light was meant to be openly displayed, not hidden. Thomas Edison's light bulbs were still almost 1900 years away and when the sun went down, lamps were essential.

When we consider this metaphor of a lamp, it becomes clear that Jesus is calling us to reflect on how we respond to His teachings and the light He brings into our lives. Are we allowing His truth to shine brightly or are we concealing it? The Scripture encourages us to recognize the transformative power of God's word in our lives. When we embrace the light of Christ, we are called not only to receive it for ourselves but also to share it with others. Just as a lamp provides guidance in darkness, our faith can illuminate the paths of those around us.

It's so easy to let fear, doubt, or societal pressures dim our light. We may hesitate to express our faith in conversations or to step into roles where we can share God's love. Jesus challenges us to overcome these obstacles and to boldly display the light we have received.

LIGHT UP: On a scale of 1 to 10, how bright am I shining my light for Jesus?

Let's live in a way that showcases God's truth and actively shine our light in the world. May each interaction give us the opportunity to reflect Christ's love and truth, encouraging others to seek the light for themselves. May we commit to being vessels of His light, allowing it to shine through our words and actions. In doing so, we fulfill our purpose as followers of Christ, illuminating the world with His grace and truth.

Reading for Reflection: Genesis 1:14-19; Luke 12:35-40

A life is not important except in the
impact it has on other lives.
Jackie Robinson

◇◇◇

TRUST AND OBEY

Why do you involve me?

John 2:4

Moms are special, especially my mom. Growing up she taught me the little chorus *Trust and Obey*, but more important than the song was the way she demonstrated that for me and my siblings. Though she experienced some of life's greatest pain, she was a person who trusted God and did her best to obey Him.

The exchange between Jesus and His earthly mother, Mary, that leads to this question of involvement is not particularly cordial (see John 2:1-12). In fact, I read this wedding reception story and find myself surprised at how Jesus responds to His mom. He tells her that the absence of wine is not His issue and the timing is not right. Notice what she does. She flat-out ignores what He says. Has your mom ever done that to you? My Mom did it to me on a pretty regular basis. I call it "selective listening." In other words, I heard you, but you failed to hear me, so think about it a little longer.

Apparently, Jesus did that and He decided that she was right. It was the right time. He had the ability to do something. His mom wanted him to act and so He did. Though I am tempted to focus on the amazing miracle of turning water in stone jars into wine, I believe this passage of Scripture is all about trust and trust can't be microwaved. It is developed over time. Mary knew Jesus. This was the woman who had changed his diapers, rocked him to sleep, fixed his meals, took him to the synagogue, and went looking for him when she thought he was lost. She trusted him to be able to do something in this situation where friends were about to be embarrassed because the wedding reception was running short on liquid refreshments. Hanging on the wall of my office are the words of John 2:5, Mary's simple response to Jesus' question…

Do whatever He tells you.

My mom chose this as a life verse for me. She wanted me to trust… and obey.

LIGHT UP: Do I trust God with all of my heart and has this trust led to obedience?

My best advice: choose trust. It will grow, develop, and mature over time. Mary knew Jesus and though I don't think she could be sure what He would do in the moment, she trusted Him. Though you may have big questions, giant concerns, or a host of doubts, start with trust and choose obedience. Do whatever He tells you.

Reading for Reflection: Psalms 20:7; Acts 5:17-29

It is not hard to obey when we love
the one whom we obey.
Saint Ignatius

◇◇◇

CONVERSATION STARTERS

Will you give me a drink?

John 4:7

A trip to Uganda fulfilled a dream on my very short bucket list. Though it was a country I knew nothing about growing up and would struggle to identify on a map, Uganda provided me an opportunity to see the power of entrepreneurship in providing clean water and business opportunities for an impoverished country. Drinking out of a garden hose as a kid, washing my car with clean water as a teenager, and being a guy who always preferred plain water to the latest cola, I was guilty of taking this American staple for granted. As an adult, I traveled to third-world countries and witnessed first-hand primarily children and women walking miles to collect water I would never consider touching for their daily cooking and drinking needs. Did you know that approximately 1.5 million people die each year from waterborne illnesses, according to estimates from the World Health Organization (WHO)? These illnesses, which include diseases like cholera, typhoid fever, and dysentery, often result from contaminated drinking water, inadequate sanitation, and poor hygiene practices. We can explore outer space, spend billions on wars, and get hot pizza delivered in less than 30 minutes, but we can't provide clean water in every part of the world?

Jesus is the living water, and his seemingly simple request to a surprised Samaritan woman opened the door to a deep conversation about spiritual thirst and the transformative power of living water (see John 4:1-26). Water is a fundamental necessity for life. It quenches our physical thirst and sustains our bodies. Jesus uses the metaphor of water to illustrate our spiritual needs. Just as our bodies require hydration, our souls crave the refreshing and fulfilling presence of God. The woman, initially focused on the physical aspect of water, soon realizes that Jesus is offering her something far greater – eternal life and spiritual nourishment.

LIGHT UP: Am I open to a divine appointment today with someone who is dying of thirst for living water?

Let us take a quick spiritual inventory. Are we trying to satisfy our spiritual hunger with temporary solutions? Are we allowing the distractions of daily life to keep us from the true source of fulfillment? Jesus stands ready to refresh us, offering His love, grace, and purpose. In moments of weariness or dryness, may we remember to draw near to Him. Let us seek the living water that sustains our spirits, invites us into deeper relationship, and empowers us to live fully in His presence. Embrace the promise of this living water, and allow it to flow through you, bringing life and hope to those around you.

Reading for Reflection: Isaiah 55; John 7:38

When the well is dry, we'll know the worth of water.
Benjamin Franklin

◇◇◇

SEEN

What is your name?

Mark 5:9

People who are great at remembering names have always impress-ed me. Psychologists tell us that people generally like hearing their own name because it triggers a sense of recognition and valida-tion. When someone addresses us by name, it signals attention and respect, indicating that the speaker is engaging with us directly. This direct engagement can make us feel valued, seen, and connected to the person speaking. Do you remember the question *"What's in a name?"* famously posed by Juliet in Shakespeare's *Romeo and Juliet*? While Juliet suggests a name is merely a label, a superficial designation, the reality is far richer and more complex. We like hearing our names called. I see that repeatedly as I watch the faces of graduates walk across the stage to receive their diplomas. When their name is announced, and family and friends in the crowd begin to cheer, I love seeing the look on their faces. It is a powerful moment.

The Gospel of Mark records a powerful moment in Jesus' ministry: a man possessed by many demons begs Jesus, "What do you want with me, Jesus, Son of the Most High God? In God's name don't torture me!" (see Mark 5:1-20) This desperate plea, uttered by a man tormented by an overwhelming spiritual force, reveals the unrelenting power of faith, even in the face of unimaginable suffering. The man, living among the tombs, was tormented by legions of demons, illustrating a life con-sumed by spiritual darkness and despair. His condition was far beyond physical ailment; it was a state of utter hopelessness and alienation. Yet, even in this desperate state, an undeniable faith emerges. The man recognizes Jesus's identity – Son of the Most High God – and pleads for mercy. This acknowledgment, despite his torment, shows the power of faith to pierce through darkness.

In the midst of this man's cry for deliverance, Jesus asks for his name. Jesus wanted to hear the man say his name. He wanted a personal connection with him because Jesus was about to change his life forever. In fact, the change was so profound that the man wanted to go with Him, to become one of his followers. But Jesus believed there was a more important work for this healed and redeemed man. Jesus asked him to go tell his story to others so that they too might believe in the power and promises of God.

LIGHT UP: Do I recognize the power of Christ in my life and the lives of others, even when we face overwhelming challenges? Can I follow Jesus' example of calling people by name so they may feel seen, connected, and loved?

This story invites us to reflect on our own faith and our capacity for belief. Like the demon-possessed man, we may find ourselves struggling with spiritual battles that seem insurmountable. Yet, in our moments of despair, we can find strength in faith, clinging to Jesus' name and recognizing His power to bring healing and transformation.

May we be inspired to embrace faith, even in the face of overwhelming difficulties. Let's recognize and claim the power of Jesus' name, knowing that He is able to set us free from the spiritual forces that bind us and bring healing to our souls. May we look for people to call by name today.

Reading for Reflection: 1 Kings 18:20-39; John 10:3

Carve your name on hearts, not on marble.
Charles Spurgeon

◇◇◇

RAPID FIRE

*Why are you talking about
having no bread? Do you still not
see or understand? Are your hearts
hardened? Do you have eyes but fail
to see, and ears but fail to hear?
And don't you remember?*

Mark 8:17-18

Police detectives ask lots of questions, it is the nature of the assignment. As a homicide detective with the Houston Police Department, I embraced the challenge of the interview, whether it was a witness or a suspect. Asking questions of strangers is far different than interrogating a friend, but I discovered that asking one question at a time and patiently waiting for a response got the best results. Jesus took a little different approach in Mark 8 as He strung together a list of questions in rapid-fire succession, each one a little more challenging than the previous.

The disciples had just witnessed the feeding of the 4,000, a miraculous event where Jesus multiplied a few loaves and fish to feed thousands (see Mark 8:14-21). Yet, in the face of their current situation – having only one loaf of bread – concern arose. Jesus knew their thoughts and pointed out their lack of awareness regarding His power and provision. This serves as a powerful reminder that we can often miss the significance of what God is doing in our lives due to our worries and distractions. The questions were not as much about bread as they were about a propensity for spiritual blindness that can sometimes cloud our understanding, even when we are in the presence of the miraculous.

Jesus' questions challenge us to reflect on our spiritual awareness. Are we so focused on our immediate problems that we fail to recognize God's presence and His faithfulness? Just like the disciples, we may have *"eyes that do not see"* and *"ears that do not hear"* when it comes to the ways God has provided for us in the past. In times of uncertainty, it is crucial to remember the miracles and blessings we have experienced. Keeping a record of God's faithfulness can strengthen our faith when we face new challenges. Let us not allow our hearts to harden against the truth of His provision.

LOOK UP: Are there areas where I struggle to see God at work in my life? Can I make a list of all the times I am certain God acted on my behalf in the past and review it from time to time for encouragement?

Discouraging news, dark times, and disappointment can dull our hearing, dim our eyesight, and cause us to forget God's faithfulness in days gone by. Dig into His Word, read until you find a verse that speaks directly to you, pray for clarity and understanding, and remember that He who provided before will provide again. May our ears be opened to His voice and may our eyes see His goodness as we trust in His unfailing love.

Reading for Reflection: 1 Chronicles 29:13-20; Philippians 4:19

> *Be assured, if you walk with Him*
> *and look to Him, and expect help from Him,*
> *He will never fail you.*
> **George Mueller**

◇◇◇

I KNOW YOU

Who do people say I am? But what
about you? Who do you say I am?

Mark 8:27, 29

Jesus asked three questions in rapid-fire succession (see Mark 8:27-30). Simon Peter, often the spokesman for the group, speaks up and says with confidence: "You are the Messiah!" Great answer and it would have been a terrific time to drop the mic and remain quiet for the rest of the conversation. You may remember the story; Jesus begins to share with the disciples what will happen to him soon. Jesus talks about how he will be rejected, killed, and resurrected in three days. Why did He tell the disciples about this in advance? He wanted them to go from seeing to seeing more clearly. They weren't blind, but they couldn't see what was ahead. Scripture tells us that Simon Peter pulled Jesus off to the side and began to rebuke Him. Can you imagine rebuking Jesus? But before we are too hard on Simon Peter, how many times have you thought you saw things clearly, only to discover that there was more to the story, more to learn?   Anyone reading these words who would like a do-over about something in your past? We all do!

Mark gives us 13 stories of such encounters. Most of these conversations are with his disciples, sometimes with the whole team, but other times with only a few; but there are also meetings with crowds, a father and a son, with a group of Pharisees, with a group of children, and with a wealthy young man. These moments and interactions with Jesus had at least two things in common:

1. Jesus asked questions – 24 questions, in fact!

2. Jesus was working with people who could SEE, but they could not SEE CLEARLY.

These 24 questions from Jesus were clarifying questions, defining moment questions. They were questions, I believe, designed to take people from seeing to seeing more clearly.

LIGHT UP: If asked today, how would I answer the question, who is Jesus to me?

As I spend time in God's Word reading the stories, as I listen to others tell their stories, and as I reflect on my own life, I've come to believe that many, if not most, of the defining moments in life come when God confronts me with a question. Sometimes, the question is one for which I have no answer. Often the question confronts me, stops me in my tracks, causes me to become silent, or maybe makes me talk too much.

Let's be quiet enough, still enough, and listen carefully enough to hear the question He might be asking today.

Reading for Reflection: Jeremiah 23:5; Philippians 2:1-11

Did I offer peace today? Did I bring a smile to someone's face? Did I say words of healing? Did I let go of my anger and resentment? Did I forgive? Did I love? These are the real questions. I must trust that the little bit of love that I sow now will bear many fruits, here in this world and the life to come.
Henri Nouwen

◇◇◇

ANCHOR DEEP

Where is your faith?

Luke 8:25

G rowing up a few blocks from the Atlantic Ocean, we had our share of hurricanes. As a kid, I thought it was exciting because my mom let me sleep in the closet. It was supposed to be the safest place in the house. Now that I'm older, I have a healthy respect for big storms, but I've retained a love for stories about storms, like this one. It was a holiday weekend back in 1979, while the rest of the country was celebrating, Hurricane David was bearing down on the Florida coast. A group of single guys were trying to figure out how to tie their houseboat to ride out the storm. They had only owned the boat for three months. They got all the rope they could locate and began to fasten the boat to everything they could find to tie on to: trees, docks, anything! One of the guys described the scene like a rerun from *McHale's Navy*. When they had used up all their rope and surveyed their work, it looked a little like a spider's web. An old timer came along and laughed at what they had done. He said:

Boys, your only hope is to anchor deep,
leave the rope slack, and pray for the best!

Pretty good advice for hurricanes and the storms of life. When the disciples found themselves in the middle of a thunderstorm (see Luke 8:22-25), Jesus asked them one of life's most basic questions. Awakened from His sleep, Jesus' question provided another teaching moment about the nature of faith, the challenges of life, and the unwavering presence of Christ. The disciples, many of who were seasoned fishermen, found themselves terrified by the storm's fury. Their fear, born from the immediate threat of drowning, overshadowed their faith. They were overwhelmed by the power of the storm, losing sight of the power of the One who was with them. This human experience of fear clouding faith is relatable; we often face situations that seem insurmountable, causing our worries to overwhelm our trust in God.

Jesus' question, *"Where is your faith?"* was not a condemnation but a call to refocus. He was not questioning the existence of their faith but challenging them to actively rely on it during the storm. It reminds us that faith is not a passive acceptance of beliefs but an active trust in God's power, even in the midst of adversity. We need "now" faith, activated and on display so others can see and be encouraged.

LIGHT UP: When confronted with difficult situations – whether financial struggles, health crises, or relational problems – do I allow fear to consume me, or do I actively rely on my faith in God? Where is my faith when the storms of life rage around me? Am I allowing fear to overwhelm me, or am I actively trusting in God's power?

May we cultivate a deeper faith, one that enables us to remain steadfast through adversity, remembering that even in the fiercest storms, Jesus is with us, He is very aware of our situation and our need, and He is capable of calming the waves. Anchor deep, pray big, and trust the Savior!

Reading for Reflection: Psalms 57:1-11; Hebrews 11:1

When the storms of life come, if they come
to me personally, to my family or to the world, I want to
be strong enough to stand and be a strength to
somebody else, be shelter for somebody else.
Anne Graham Lotz

◇◇◇

SHINING BRIGHT

Are there not twelve hours of daylight?

John 11:9

"This Little Light of Mine" is a favorite song for me. Growing up I have fond memories of belting it out and participating in all the motions associated with it. What I never knew was that it was a traditional African American gospel song that had its roots in the early 20th century. Its origins can be traced back to the Civil Rights Movement, where it became a popular anthem for empowerment and hope. The song emphasizes the importance of letting one's light shine, symbolizing the expression of individuality, faith, and resilience against oppression. The melody is simple and catchy, which has allowed it to be adapted and sung in various contexts, including children's choirs and community gatherings. Over the years, many artists have recorded their versions, further cementing its place in American music and culture.

Jesus asked a question about daylight at what appeared to be a most inconvenient and odd time (see John 11:1-44). His friend Lazarus has died, and He is in the process of slowly returning to Bethany, a place where the Jews had tried to stone Him. At the time, the disciples were unaware that they were about to witness as big a miracle as can be imagined, a resurrection from the dead.

The imagery of light and darkness serves as a rich metaphor and one Jesus used to help the disciples, and us, understand His mission and the way we should navigate our lives. Jesus emphasizes the importance of walking in the light, which symbolizes living in alignment with God's truth and purpose. In the physical sense, walking in the daylight allows us to see clearly, avoiding the pitfalls and dangers that lurk in the shadows.

Spiritually, walking in the light means remaining in relationship with Christ, who is the light of the world (John 8:12). It is through Him that we gain clarity, direction, and the ability to avoid the stumbling blocks of sin and despair. The question Jesus asked His disciples invites us to reflect on how we are living our lives.

LIGHT UP: Are we choosing to walk in the light of Christ, or are we allowing the darkness of doubt, fear, and sin to lead us astray?

The assurance that we will not stumble when we walk in the light speaks to the protective nature of God's guidance. He desires for us to live fully in His presence, experiencing the safety and joy that comes with it. As we consider the question of daylight hours from the verse above, let us commit to walking in the light by seeking God's wisdom through prayer, Scripture, and community. In doing so, we will find the strength to pursue His calling and navigate the challenges of life with confidence. Remember, in Christ, we have the light that dispels darkness and leads us to a fulfilling life.

Reading for Reflection: Isaiah 9:2; John 1:6-12

> *Hope is being able to see that there is*
> *light despite all of the darkness.*
> **Desmond Tutu**

◇◇◇

NAUGHTY OR NICE

What were you arguing about on the road?

Mark 9:33

Santa Claus is Coming to Town is a great reminder to little children throughout the year because of the message about jolly St. Nick seeing both the ones who are awake and asleep and the promise of the naughty and nice list he is keeping. Judge me if you must, but I've reminded my kids and now grandkids of this song in months that were nowhere close to Christmas…and it works!

In this Scripture, Jesus captures a time when His disciples were debating among themselves about who was the greatest. Can you imagine how this must have made Him feel? He teaches and preaches humility and service, and they squabble over the pettiness of position. Jesus asks a question and what does He get for an answer? Silence – you could hear a pin drop! Even Simon Peter who always had a response remains quiet, perhaps because he was at the forefront of the discussion. Jesus, undeterred by their failure to own the argument, knew their thoughts and intentions and used this opportunity to teach them a vital lesson about humility and the nature of true greatness.

The disciples' argument reveals a common human tendency: the desire for status, recognition, and superiority. In their quest for importance, they overlooked the calling to serve and love one another. Jesus, aware of their hearts, does not condemn them outright but gently guides them toward a better understanding of His Kingdom.

In response to their arguments, Jesus emphasizes that greatness in His Kingdom is not measured by power or prestige, but by humility and service. He often turned societal norms upside down, showing that the first shall be last, and the greatest shall be the servant of all (Mark 9:35). This teaching invites us to reflect on our own lives.

LIGHT UP: Am I seeking recognition or striving to serve others?

True greatness in the eyes of God is found in our willingness to lower ourselves for the benefit of others. It's about putting aside our egos and ambitions to embrace a posture of humility. When we serve others selflessly, we reflect the heart of Christ, who came not to be served but to serve (Mark 10:45).

May we learn to value others above ourselves and seek opportunities to serve rather than to be served. In doing so, we align ourselves with the teachings of Jesus and become true ambassadors of His love and grace in a world that often prizes self-promotion over selflessness.

Reading for Reflection: Daniel 1:3-20; 2 Corinthians 10:12-18

Those who are happiest are those who do the most for others.
Booker T. Washington

◇◇◇

GET UP

I tell you, get up,
take your mat and go home.

Mark 2:11

Reckless Friends - Mark 2:8

Don't Blink - Mark 13:2

Pledging Allegiance - Matthew 17:25

Lost, But Someone's Looking - Matthew 18:12

Expectations - Mark 10:36

Cost Accounting - Luke 14:31

Undaunted Courage - John 18:4, 7

Looking for a Fight - Matthew 26:55

Dry Season - Luke 23:31

◇◇◇

RECKLESS FRIENDS

Why are you thinking these things?

Mark 2:8

Do you have a 4:00 am friend? Are you a 4:00 am friend? 4:00 am friends are those who you could call in the middle of the night, and they would not only answer the phone but also get up and come to your assistance regardless of the expense or inconvenience the trip would require. The paralyzed man in Mark 2 had not one or two or even three 4:00 am friends, he had at least four and they demonstrated their love and loyalty to him in the most remarkable way (see Mark 2:1-12).

Their bold, extravagant, and perhaps somewhat reckless response leads us to an important question Jesus asks some religious teachers gathered to hear Him when His teaching is interrupted by a newly created hole in the roof. Jesus knew what these learned scholars were thinking and their concern that He had forgiven sins and almost as if to say, "you ain't seen nothing yet." Jesus goes on to command the man to get up, take up his mat, and walk. Healed inside and outside in the midst of a crowd and I've always wondered if Jesus patched the roof too!

Do you remember whose faith had created the opportunity for the healing? It is my favorite part of the story. Scripture tells us it was the faith of the friends. Wow, don't you want friends like that loving you, lifting you, investing in your life? While this story may highlight the divine power of Jesus, it also underscores the importance of having great friends. They were determined and when they faced obstacles – a crowded house and no way to get through – they didn't give up. Instead, they creatively devised a risky plan to lower their friend through the roof. The healing doesn't happen without their determination and faith.

Great friends go beyond casual companionship. They actively support and uplift one another in times of need. Just as these friends showed unwavering commitment, we are reminded of the value of surrounding ourselves with those who inspire us to pursue Christ. In moments of struggle, doubt, or paralysis – whether emotional, spiritual, or physical – having friends who believe in us and in God's power can transform our experiences.

GET UP: Am I going the extra mile to demonstrate my love and commitment to others?

This story challenges and convicts me. They didn't wait for their friend to find a way to Jesus alone; they took initiative. Can we accept the call to be proactive in our friendships, encouraging others to seek healing and hope in Christ? As you reflect on your own friendships, consider how you can be a great friend to others. Are you willing to risk, to lift someone up when they are down, and to bring them to Jesus? May we strive to cultivate relationships that lead us and our friends closer to Him.

Reading for Reflection: Ecclesiastes 4:9-10; Galatians 6:1-10

A real friend is one who walks in
when the rest of the world walks out.
Walter Winchell

◇◇◇

DON'T BLINK

Do you see all these great buildings?

Mark 13:2

Walking through the World Trade Center in 1992 and then taking the elevator to the observation center high above New York City, I was certain this was the most amazing structure I had ever visited. Skyscrapers have always left me in awe and wonder. How are they designed and constructed in ways that create cities within cities and feature lights, air conditioning, heating, and plumbing that serve so many people 24 hours a day and 365 days a year? If the world was dependent upon me to design and build these monstrosities, I think we might all still be living in caves or lean-tos!

The disciples were struck by the grandeur and magnificence of the Temple, and Jesus uses this moment to remind them – and us – of the temporary nature of earthly things (see Mark 13:1-8). The Temple in Jerusalem was the center of Jewish life and worship, a symbol of stability and permanence. Yet, Jesus points to its future destruction, illustrating that even the most seemingly secure and magnificent things can be transient. This verse invites us to reflect on what we place our trust and value in - is it temporary or eternal? Be assured it matters.

It seems so easy for us to get caught up in the pursuit of material possessions, status, and achievements. We are often tempted to strive for success, believing it will bring lasting fulfillment. However, as Jesus teaches, these pursuits can be fleeting. True security and meaning cannot be found in the things of this world, as they are ultimately temporary.

Instead, we are called to focus on what is eternal – the love of God, our relationships with others, and the impact we can have on the world around us. Investing in faith, kindness, and service creates a legacy that endures beyond our earthly existence.

GET UP: Am I investing in eternal things or those that ultimately do not last?

Here's a great moment to pause and evaluate our priorities. Are we building our lives on the solid foundation of Christ, who offers us eternal hope and purpose? May we remember that while earthly structures may crumble, our faith in God remains steadfast. Let us choose to invest in what truly matters, ensuring that our lives reflect the light and love of Jesus in a world that often prioritizes the temporary.

Reading for Reflection: Nehemiah 8:1-18; 2 Corinthians 4:18

> *Between temporal and eternal things there is this difference:*
> *a temporal thing is loved more before we have it, and it*
> *begins to grow worthless when we gain it, for it does not*
> *satisfy the soul, whose true and certain rest is eternity;*
> *but the eternal is more ardently loved when it is*
> *acquired than when it is merely desired.*
> **Augustine of Hippo**

◇◇◇

PLEDGING ALLEGIANCE

What do you think, Simon?
From whom do the kings of the earth
collect duty and taxes – from their
own children or from others?

Matthew 17:25

O nce upon a time and one time only, I completed my own tax return without any help. A subsequent audit revealed that I had made a mistake and listed a credit as a debit leading me to pay additional tax and a penalty. Since that time, wisdom has ruled the day. I have chosen to invest in the experience and expertise of others to complete my tax return. While I'm a faithful taxpayer, I'm grateful that God did not call me to be a tax preparer.

In a letter dated November 13, 1789, Benjamin Franklin wrote, *"Our new Constitution is now established, and has an appearance that promises permanency; but in this world nothing can be said to be certain, except death and taxes."* Jesus understood the reality of death and the necessity of taxes though He shared a message that promised a day would come when we could live forever, tax-free. But in our current state, we pay taxes often, which creates lots of conversation and employment for many people.

The setting for the question Jesus poses to Simon Peter is significant (see Matthew 17:24-27). He and His disciples are in Capernaum, and the temple tax collectors approached Peter. The tax, a half-shekel, was levied on every adult Jewish male to support the Temple in Jerusalem. Jesus, though divine, demonstrates His humanity by instructing Peter to pay the tax, highlighting His submission to earthly authorities. However, the subsequent question to Peter is far more profound than a simple instruction on financial matters.

By asking whose image appears on the coins, Jesus directs Peter's attention to the authority and power that the coins represent. While the coins bore the image of Caesar, the Roman emperor, symbolizing the political and economic control Rome held over Judea, Jesus' question is not about the tax itself but about allegiance and identity. Whose authority do we truly acknowledge? Whose image do we bear?

Jesus instructs Peter to pay the tax and gives instructions about where he can find the required coin. Peter, the fisherman, secures the four-drachma-required coin in the mouth of the first fish he catches. (I love this part of the story!) Jesus was not condoning Roman oppression but demonstrating His decision to submit to earthly authority while at the same time revealing the ultimate authority of God. He pays the tax, fulfilling the earthly requirement, yet the miracle underscores who is really in control.

GET UP: Do I bear the image of Christ and does my life demonstrate allegiance through complete surrender to Him?

Jesus' question is a call to self-examination. It challenges us to evaluate our priorities, to identify the true source of our identity, and to ensure our lives reflect our commitment to Him. May we seek to align our lives with God's will. Let's prioritize His kingdom above all earthly pursuits, recognizing that true wealth, true power, and true honor come from Him alone. May our actions reflect our allegiance to Christ, showing through our lives the image of the one who truly reigns.

Reading for Reflection: Psalms 40:1-5; Hebrews 13:15-17

The best things in life are tax free.
Joseph Bonkowski

◇◇◇

LOST, BUT SOMEONE'S LOOKING

*What do you think? If a man owns
a hundred sheep, and one of them
wanders away, will he not leave the
ninety-nine on the hills and go to look
for the one that wandered off?*

Matthew 18:12

How do you feel about 99%? Math was not my best subject in school, but I learned the basics, and I learned something about percentages. For example, 99% is a tremendous score on a school assignment... it would keep almost every parent happy, it is an excellent return on investment, and any team would be ecstatic about winning 99% of their games. The truth is that 99% would be acceptable almost all the time. I say almost because you would demand changes if only 99% of the planes landed safely daily at your local airport. I'm guessing more than a few of you would be upset if your youth pastor only brought back 99% of the teens who went to camp. Jesus had a major problem with only 99%. He didn't buy into the theory that a "bird in the hand is worth more than two in the bush."

Have you ever lost anything really valuable? I'm guessing we all have stories we could tell. Some of us who have the gift of losing things could write our own book. I once lost my car in a parking lot, not a parking garage - lots of people have done that. I lost mine in a parking lot and it wasn't even that big a parking lot! Sometimes you lose something, and you have no idea where you lost it. To me, the most frustrating times are when I lose something and I know it is right there, close by, somewhere in my office or my house, but I just can't seem to find it. I've discovered that my level of anxiety and the intensity of my search are in direct proportion to the value of the object I've lost.

Jesus made a big deal about lost people. This simple question He asks (see Matthew 18:12-14) reveals an overwhelming truth about God's love, His relentless pursuit of His lost children, and the importance of compassion and forgiveness. The parable of the lost sheep illustrates God's unwavering commitment to seeking and saving those who are lost. The shepherd, representing Jesus, leaves the ninety-nine sheep – symbolizing those who already follow Him – to search for the one lost sheep. This act demonstrates the immeasurable value of each individual in God's eyes. No one is insignificant; each person is precious enough to warrant a dedicated search. The shepherd's relentless pursuit is a powerful reflection of God's love for every person, regardless of their past mistakes or current struggles.

GET UP: Am I willing to go the extra mile to seek out those who are lost, extending compassion, forgiveness, and understanding? Do I focus solely on those within my established circles, neglecting the needs of those who are outside or have fallen away?

Jesus' question challenges us to examine our own hearts and our attitudes toward those who have strayed from the faith or who are struggling in their lives. May we be empowered to reach out, offering help and support to those who are struggling, remembering that each person is precious in God's sight and worthy of our love and concern. Let us embrace the challenge to seek out the lost, reflecting the boundless love of our Good Shepherd.

Reading for Reflection: Ezekiel 37:11-14; 1 Corinthians 1:18

God uses rescued people to rescue people.
Christine Caine

◇◇◇

EXPECTATIONS

What do you want me to do for you?

Mark 10:36

The story of Bartimaeus reminds me of a play written by Samuel Beckett. The title of the play is "Waiting for Godot." In the play, two tramps in baggy pants and bowler hats, Vladimir and Estagon, stand at the side of a country road, day after day, waiting for the mysterious character of Godot. Their wait forms the whole play.

No one seems to know who this Godot is…only that everything depends on his coming. *"If Godot comes, 'we'll be saved,'* goes a line at the end. But slowly the truth sinks in. Godot isn't coming! Still, the men go on waiting in a strange, hopeless hope that at times is too unbearable to watch. Vladimir and Estagon, in their tramplike, almost clownish clothes, seem to be a part of some sad cosmic joke. As the play ends, they're still waiting. Godot hasn't come. Some have suggested that Godot stands for God, or at least humanity's hope for someone who would come and give everything meaning.

Perhaps much of the Christian life and ministry is about living in the in-between – that gap between God's call on our life and that day when we will meet Him in glory. But if we are honest, waiting is hard for most of us.

The question is, how do we wait? How do we deal with the frustration of what we expect and what we've got? Whether it is our marriage, our children, our careers – how do we wait on God to do what we think He ought to do? And can we be still and patient?

My wife and I have a restaurant that we visit on a semi-regular basis. It is a pretty popular place. In fact, I don't believe we have ever walked right in and been seated. We were there once and were told there would be a ninety-minute wait, and we waited! The hostess in this restaurant always gives us this little square electronic device with a single blinking red light. We waited so long one time that I began to ponder why the little red light blinked. The only conclusion I could come up with was that it lets you know the device is working.

Watching people's reaction to the flashing lights and vibrating pager would make you think that something exciting had happened in their life as opposed to just being seated at a table in a restaurant! I once conducted my own little sociological study as I waited. Some people squealed when their wait was over. Other people dropped the pager they were so excited. There were a few people who kind of held it UP, almost as if they were *taunting* those of us who were still waiting. Waiting for a table in a restaurant is EXPECTANT waiting. But you wait expectantly!

I think that is how God wants us to wait for Him. We wait with expectation, absolutely convinced that in His time, He will act, and we can trust Him.

GET UP: How am I waiting?

God invites us to rest in His presence, to be confident in His Word, to lean in and lean on Him. He promises to go before us. He is our shield of faith. We can trust Him with every detail of our life and walk through this day assured that He is for us!

Reading for Reflection: Micah 7:7; 1 John 4:16

True worship is open to God, adoring God,
waiting for God, trusting God even in the dark.
N.T. Wright

◇◇◇

COST ACCOUNTING

*Or suppose a king is about to go to war
against another king. Won't he first sit down and consider
whether he is able with ten thousand men to oppose
the one coming against him with twenty thousand?*

Luke 14:31

You've probably heard the old adage: *failing to plan is planning to fail.* Though it often appeared that Jesus operated without a plan, nothing could be further from the truth. His arrival in a manger of Bethlehem was part of a plan that pre-dates creation. While planning consumes a great deal of my time, I've seen its value repeatedly over the years. And while some might argue that planning reveals a lack of faith, I would strongly disagree. Great planning is a step of faith that expresses confidence in God's blessing upon the dream being pursued.

Jesus asks another question in a discourse with a large crowd that was following Him (see Luke 14:31-33). As a little side note, have you ever noticed that Jesus seems to make statements and ask questions that thin out the congregation? I wonder if there isn't a message there for us about watering down the gospel. The question posed to His followers on that day highlights the importance of preparation, wisdom, and the necessity of counting the cost before pursuing big endeavors. He uses this metaphor of soldiers and battle to illustrate the seriousness of discipleship. Just as a king must evaluate his resources and strategy before going to war, we too, must assess our commitment and readiness to follow Christ. Discipleship is not a casual decision; it requires intentionality, sacrifice, and a willingness to face challenges.

In our rapid and, at times, reckless world, we often rush into decisions without fully considering the implications. Whether it's a career change, a relationship, or a commitment to spiritual growth, taking time to reflect and prepare can lead to more fruitful outcomes. Jesus encourages us to be thoughtful and deliberate in our pursuits, ensuring we align our goals with His will.

GET UP: Am I considering a change in life that has not been bathed in prayer and blessed with wise counsel from a mentor?

While we may feel inadequate to make some of the decisions before us, we must remember that our power comes from Him. We are not called to face life's battles alone; God equips us with the wisdom and resources we need to navigate challenges. Let us commit to being wise stewards of our lives. May we take the time to pray, seek counsel, and evaluate our commitments. In doing so, we can step forward with confidence, knowing that we are prepared for the journey ahead. Embracing this wisdom allows us to pursue our calling with clarity and purpose, trusting in God's guidance every step of the way.

Reading for Reflection: Proverbs 20:18; Galatians 5:22-26

The quieter you become, the more you hear.
Anonymous

◇◇◇

UNDAUNTED COURAGE

Who is it you want?

John 18:4,7

As a history major I love reading the stories of exploration and discovery. Near the top of my list of favorite books is *Undaunted Courage* by Stephen Ambrose, the story of Meriwether Lewis, William Clark, and their small team known as the Corp of Discovery. Their assignment was to explore the Missouri River westward in an attempt to find a water passage to the Pacific Ocean. The group faced challenges, setbacks, disease, and starvation, but they continued on, and Ambrose chose a great title for his book, for their courage appeared to have been undaunted. As I read the book, I asked myself the question: If I had been alive at that time (1804-1806), would I have signed up for such a risky expedition? Do I have that kind of courage? What about you? Do you consider yourself a person of great courage?

Jesus possessed something far beyond undaunted courage. Scripture tells us (see John 18:1-9) that when he had finished praying, He left with his disciples and crossed the Kidron Valley. On the other side was a garden, and He and His disciples went into it. Judas, who would betray Him, also knew the place, because Jesus had often met there with his disciples. So, Judas came to the garden, guiding a detachment of soldiers and some officials from the chief priests and the Pharisees. They were carrying torches, lanterns, and weapons. Jesus, knowing all that was going to happen to Him, went out and asked them, *"Who is it you want?"* *"Jesus of Nazareth,"* they replied. *"I am He,"* Jesus said. (And Judas the traitor was standing there with them.) When Jesus said, *"I am He,"* they drew back and fell to the ground. Again, He asked them, *"Who is it you want?" "Jesus of Nazareth,"* they said. Jesus answered, *"I told you that I am He. If you are looking for me, then let these men go."* This happened so that the words He had spoken would be fulfilled: *"I have not lost one of those you gave me."*

The garden, a place of intimacy where Jesus frequently prayed with His disciples, becomes the scene of betrayal. Jesus' knowledge of what lay ahead – arrest, torture, and crucifixion – did not deter Him. Instead, He stepped forward and addressed His captors with courage and resolve knowing that this was all part of God's plan. He would go willingly to the cross for your sins and mine.

GET UP: What is my response when I am mistreated, maybe even betrayed? Is there an issue I am currently facing that requires courage and have I considered the impact my response can have on others?

Like Jesus, we all face moments of trial and tribulation, and in these moments, we may feel overwhelmed, anxious, or betrayed. We are called to respond with the same courage that Jesus exhibited knowing that nothing can separate us from the love of God in Christ Jesus. When we confront our fears, we can trust that God is with us and for us. Jesus' example teaches us to acknowledge our circumstances without being defined by them. Because of Him, we too, can have undaunted courage.

Reading for Reflection: Deuteronomy 31:6; Romans 8:37-39

For what is faith unless it is to believe what you do not see?
Saint Augustine

◇◇◇

LOOKING FOR A FIGHT

Am I leading a rebellion,
that you have come out with
swords and clubs to capture me?

Matthew 26:55

O ne of the most exciting and dangerous times for police officers is executing an arrest warrant. The response of the individual to be arrested is unpredictable, some people come along peacefully while others are itching for a fight. Some of my most memorable moments were capturing criminals and securing them safely in jail to await trial for the crimes for which they had been accused.

Jesus was no criminal, but He was arrested in the garden of Gethsemane and He addressed the crowd that had come to seize Him with a question, and then gave this response:

Every day I sat in the temple courts teaching,
and you did not arrest me. But this has all taken place
that the writings of the prophets might be fulfilled.
Matthew 26:55-56

This statement captures a moment of profound irony and authority, revealing both the nature of Christ's mission and the misunderstanding of those around Him. Jesus had been openly teaching and performing miracles in the very heart of Jerusalem (see Matthew 26:47-56). His message was one of love, grace, and redemption, yet the response from the religious leaders was one of violence and hostility. In His calm reaction, Jesus underscores that He was not a threat to the established order, nor was He leading a rebellion against Rome. Instead, He was fulfilling the prophecies and purposes of God, even in the face of betrayal and imminent suffering.

So, while none of us are arresting officers for Jesus, what can this question teach us? Could we be challenged to reflect on how we perceive authority in our own lives? In a world often marked by chaos and conflict, we may be tempted to respond with fear or aggression. But Jesus models a different approach – one rooted in peace and trust in God's plan. He willingly submitted to arrest, knowing that His path led to the cross and ultimately to our salvation.

GET UP: Am I responding to challenges with faith and composure, or am I allowing fear to dictate my actions?

Jesus' example encourages us to stand firm in our beliefs, even when faced with opposition, and to trust in God's greater purpose for our circumstances. Ultimately, Matthew 26:55 reminds us that Christ's authority transcends earthly powers. He is sovereign over everything, and in Him, we find peace and strength to face the storms of life.

Reading for Reflection: Proverbs 3:5-6; Titus 3:1

Perhaps nothing in our society is more needed for those in positions of authority than accountability.
Larry Burkett

◇◇◇

DRY SEASON

*For if people do these things when the tree
is green, what will happen when it is dry?*

Luke 23:31

As I write these words, all eyes have been on California and the deadly and destructive wildfires. Dry timber and high winds are a dynamic duo that has brought much pain to many people. Despite the best efforts of firefighters battling on the ground and from the air, the loss was unpreventable as the fire spread acre after acre. Watching from a distance left many feeling helpless and wondering how this could possibly be happening.

Some women of Jerusalem were mourning for Jesus as He carried the cross upon which He would be crucified, and I have to believe that they felt helpless and left wondering how could the One in whom they had put so much hope be walking this road (see Luke 23:26-34). His words offered a profound truth about the consequences of our choices and the state of our hearts. He chose the metaphor of the green tree representing His life and ministry – a time of hope, healing, and divine purpose. While He showed nothing but goodness and mercy, the people still chose to reject Him, leading to His impending crucifixion.

Jesus' question challenges us to consider the gravity of our actions and the spiritual state of our lives. This moment invites us to reflect on our own choices and the condition of our hearts. Are we living in alignment with the teachings of Jesus, or are we allowing the distractions and demands of life to pull us away from Him? Just as the green tree symbolizes life, our relationship with Christ should be vibrant and growing. Neglecting that relationship can lead to spiritual dryness, where we feel distant from God and unable to bear fruit.

GET UP: Am I in a dry spell? When was the last time I heard from God, or He heard from me? What decisions might I make in this moment to seek Him first with all my heart?

Jesus' words remind us that there is a time for decision-making. Each day, we are faced with choices that shape our faith and character. Are we choosing to follow Christ wholeheartedly, or are we allowing fear, doubt, or worldly desires to govern our actions?

Let's examine our hearts and ask God to reveal areas in our lives that need renewal. Are we nurturing our relationship with Him, seeking His guidance and wisdom in our choices? May we be encouraged to live as green trees, rooted in faith and bearing fruit in our lives. Let us embrace the challenge of following Christ, trusting that His ways lead to abundant life. In doing so, we can reflect His love and grace to a world in desperate need of hope.

Reading for Reflection: Jeremiah 17:7-8; Revelation 7:17

It is a great grace to be able to experience God's presence in our feelings and thoughts, but when we don't, it does not mean that God is absent. It often means that God is calling us to a greater faithfulness. It is precisely in times of spiritual dryness that we must hold on to our spiritual discipline so that we can grow into new intimacy with God.
Henri Nouwen

◇◇◇

LIVE UP

*Only let us live up to what we
have already attained.*

Philippians 3:16

Practicing the Way - Luke 6:46

Nic at Night - John 3:10

Expectations - Matthew 11:7-8

Compaction - Matthew 12:11

Inside Out - Mark 7:18

In Progress - Mark 8:23

Road Less Traveled - Luke 10:36

Wash Your Hands - Luke 11:40

Bold Prayers - Luke 18:8

◇◇◇

PRACTICING THE WAY

*Why do you call me, 'Lord, Lord,'
and do not do what I say?*

Luke 6:46

Bumper stickers amuse me. Though I've made it a point never to put them on a vehicle I've owned, I love to read them, and I'm convinced that you can make some initial assessments about the drivers of the vehicles based on what they choose to attach to their car. Recently I was behind an older vehicle that appeared to be held together with bumper stickers. There were so many that I'm not sure what you would learn from reading the multitude of messages other than they appeared to love (or need) bumper stickers. You've probably seen the bumper sticker that says, *"If you can read this, then you are following too close."* I'm convinced that if Jesus were driving down the street, he would not be in a vehicle with that message. In all my years of walking with Jesus, I'm convinced that you can't follow Him too closely.

Jesus' simple inquiry, delivered within the context of His teachings, reveals a powerful truth about the nature of faith and the importance of aligning our actions with our words (see Luke 6:46-49). He challenges those who may outwardly profess faith but fail to live according to His teachings. It highlights the critical distinction between merely acknowledging Jesus as Lord and actually following His commands. It is a call to examine the depth of our faith to ensure that our beliefs are reflected in our actions. Does our walk match our talk? Are we living a life of complete surrender and obedience? Jesus does not call us to a minimum standard.

In our own lives, it's easy to fall into the trap of lip service. We may attend church services, read Scripture, and engage in religious "stuff" without allowing the teachings of Christ to truly transform our hearts and actions. Jesus' question serves as a wake-up call, urging us to examine the consistency between our faith and our lives. The words "Lord, Lord," while expressing reverence and respect, are insufficient without corresponding obedience. Jesus is not interested in empty pronouncements or superficial faith; He desires a genuine relationship built on trust, obedience, and a commitment to living out His teachings. This includes acts of love, compassion, forgiveness, and service to others.

LIVE UP: Do my actions reflect my claim that Jesus is Lord? Am I living a life of obedience, love, and service, or am I simply paying lip service to my faith?

If we truly believe Jesus is Lord, our lives will reflect that belief. Our choices, our decisions, and our interactions with others will be shaped by our commitment to follow His commands. Authentic faith is not simply a matter of intellectual assent but a transformation that permeates every aspect of our lives. May we strive to align our words with our deeds, ensuring that our faith is not merely a profession but a lived reality. This involves intentional efforts to study Scripture, to pray, and to actively seek opportunities to serve others.

Reading for Reflection: Psalms 119:10; Acts 5:27-32

> *When obedience to God contradicts what I think will*
> *give me pleasure, let me ask myself if I love Him.*
> **Elisabeth Elliot**

◇◇◇

NIC AT NIGHT

You are Israel's teacher, and do you not
understand these things?

John 3:10

Thanks to millions of awesome and often forgotten Sunday School teachers, John 3:16 is the first verse we ever memorize. Two guys in American culture have helped create some interest and curiosity about John 3:16. The first guy traveled around the country for years attending major sporting events and getting on camera with his rainbow wig and John 3:16 t-shirt or sign. The second guy, Tim Tebow, once the quarterback for the University of Florida Gators and later the Denver Broncos, wore John 3:16 under his eyes stenciled in the black of the sun reflectors. Over 90 million people Googled John 3:16 as a result of this. Let that sink in for a minute: That means that 90 million people DID NOT KNOW what many of us learned as children! The rainbow wig guy is in prison serving multiple life sentences. The moral of this story is that it is not about what hangs around your neck or the bumper sticker on your car or t-shirts, it is about a relationship.

Sometimes we forget the context of the question Jesus asks in John 3, but it is offered by Jesus in the midst of a conversation with Nicodemus, a Pharisee, a teacher of the law, one of the super religious (see John 3:1-21). In this conversation, Jesus extends an invitation, one that continues to be extended even today. An invitation to believe that Jesus Christ is the Messiah, the Savior of the world.

Read the Gospel of John, and you will see a word repeated in virtually every single chapter. It is the word **BELIEVE**. Apparently, the word believe was a big deal to Jesus and an important word for John as he wrote the gospel with his name attached.

I asked AI for a Biblical definition of believe. Here is what I got:

The word "believe" means to trust in Christ as the only way to obtain eternal life with God and to be saved by him. It also means to trust in God so strongly that you are willing to commit your life to him and to personally trust him as your Lord and Savior.

Nicodemus was still struggling to believe when he encountered Jesus. As a teacher of Israel, Nicodemus was expected to grasp these profound concepts, yet he struggled to comprehend the depth of what Jesus was revealing. Belief is not merely an intellectual assent; it involves a deep trust and reliance on Jesus as the source of life and truth. Jesus emphasizes that understanding and faith go hand in hand. For us, believing in Christ means embracing who He is – our Savior, our Redeemer, and the embodiment of God's love. Without this belief, we risk living in spiritual darkness, unable to see the fullness of the life He offers.

LIVE UP: What truths about Jesus do I struggle to believe? How can I deepen my understanding of Him?

Jesus called Nicodemus to a greater understanding and invites us to deepen our faith and belief in Him. Belief in Jesus transforms our perspectives. It allows us to see beyond our circumstances to the hope and future He offers. When we believe, we are empowered to navigate challenges with confidence, knowing that God is with us and that His plans for us are good.

Reading for Reflection: Psalms 23; Romans 10:9

Belief cannot be forced. If we are bullied or seduced or manipulated to believe, we do not end up believing, we end up intimidated or used. And we are less, not more.
Eugene Peterson

◇◇◇

EXPECTATIONS

*What did you go out into the
wilderness to see? A reed swayed by
the wind? If not, what did you go out
to see? A man dressed in fine clothes?*

Matthew 11:7-8

The first university chapel of the year found me sitting in the top row of the bleachers in the gym where we met a couple of times each week during the school year. When I read the name of the opening speaker, Dr. Charles Allen, Senior Pastor of Houston's First Methodist Church, I thought he had a tough assignment before him. His audience was a tough one, college students required to attend, and at this point in his life, Dr. Allen was probably in his early 80s, or at least he seemed that old to me. When the time came for him to speak, he rose and began with a story.

I was walking near the church in downtown Houston recently when I came upon a man wearing only one shoe. When I suggested to him that he had lost a shoe he responded quickly and directly: "No sir, I found one!"

Dr. Allen went on to speak about the power of faith in your life and I'm guessing that I'm not the only one who remembers his message now four-plus decades later. Faith finds us and forms us and can sustain us, especially when life does not turn out like we expected.

John the Baptizer, cousin of Jesus, a strange-dressing prophet with an unusual diet, set-up man for Jesus, finds himself in a place he did not expect. Imprisoned and facing uncertainty about his future, he sends messengers to Jesus with a crucial question: *"Are you the one who is to come, or should we expect someone else?"* This seemingly simple inquiry reveals the depth of John's faith, his struggle with doubt, and the importance of recognizing the presence of the Messiah.

John, this powerful prophet who had prepared the way for Jesus, now finds himself in a cell, grappling with questions of identity and timing. His question is not one of disbelief but rather one of seeking confirmation and reassurance. He had proclaimed Jesus as the Lamb of God, the one who would baptize with the Holy Spirit (see John 1:29-34), yet the reality of imprisonment and uncertainty can cause even the most faithful to wrestle with doubt.

Jesus' response was not a simple "yes" or "no." Instead, He points to the works He has performed – healing the sick, raising the dead, proclaiming the good news – as evidence of His identity. Jesus does not dismiss John's doubt but guides him, and us, toward a deeper understanding of faith. Sometimes, our faith is tested, and doubt can creep into our hearts. It is in these moments that we must turn to the evidence of God's presence and power in our lives.

LIVE UP: Am I living with some unexpected realities that have led to doubts in my life? What is keeping me from taking my doubts to Jesus?

Like John, we may find ourselves in moments of questioning, seeking confirmation of God's plan for our lives. Jesus' response is a reminder that faith is not blind acceptance, but a confident trust built on evidence and relationship. The miracles and teachings of Jesus, the transformation He brings into the lives of individuals, and the power of the Holy Spirit are all evidence of His identity and authority. Remembering these moments of God's intervention in our lives and the lives of others can strengthen our faith and help us to overcome doubt.

Reading for Reflection: Psalms 55:22; 1 John 5:1-5

Faith is deliberate confidence in the character
of God whose ways you may not understand at the time.
Oswald Chambers

◇◇◇

COMPACTION

*If any of you has a sheep and it falls
into a pit on the Sabbath, will you not
take hold of it and lift it out?*

Matthew 7:16

A couple of definitions to review associated with the question Jesus asks in a confrontation with the Pharisees in Matthew 12.

COMPASSION – *"sympathy for suffering of others
often including a desire to help"*

ACTION – *"process of doing something
in order to achieve a purpose"*

Put the two words together and you get an invented word: COMPACTION. Compaction is doing more than feeling sorry for or going beyond expressing your sorrow to someone else, it is reaching out with the purpose of making things better.

- **Jesus sees the need.**
- **Jesus seizes the moment.**
- **Jesus serves.**

The Pharisees seemed to continually be at odds with Jesus about his propensity to heal on the Sabbath, a violation of the Law in their eyes. In this instance, it was the healing of a man with a withered hand. Jesus used this moment to teach about the priority of compassion over rigid adherence to the law. The Pharisees had become so focused on the rules and regulations surrounding the Sabbath that they lost sight of the heart of the law – love and mercy. Jesus' question challenges the cultural norms of His time, highlighting that compassion should always take precedence over tradition. If we would rescue a sheep in distress, how much more should we care for a fellow human being in need?

This question spurs us to reflect on our own lives. Are there times when we prioritize rules or routines over acts of kindness, or are we simply too busy, too engaged in our own agendas, or afraid that getting involved might cost us more than we are willing to invest? In our pursuit of faith, it can be easy to become legalistic or downright selfish, focusing on what is "right" rather than embodying the love of Christ. Jesus calls us to a higher standard – a standard rooted in compassion, grace, and understanding.

LIVE UP: Who am I missing in my own life that needs more than sympathy from me, they need an investment, an infusion, and they need it now?

Let us examine our hearts and ask ourselves how we can be more compassionate in our daily lives. Do we notice the needs of those around us? Are we willing to take action, even when it may disrupt our plans or challenge our comfort zones? In a world that often prioritizes efficiency and productivity, we are called to slow down and show love. May we strive to be like Jesus, who exemplified compassion and mercy at every turn. Let us be ready to lift others out of their pits, offering help and hope in their times of need. Compassion is a powerful expression of faith, and through our actions, we can reflect the heart of Christ to those around us.

Reading for Reflection: Lamentations 3:22-24; Ephesians 4:32

Hope is invented every day.
James Baldwin

◇◇◇

INSIDE OUT

Are you so dull?

Mark 7:18

Praise in public and correct in private is some advice given to me somewhere along the way. Wash your hands before you eat a meal was another maxim repeated often at our home growing up and one that we continued with our kids and now our grandkids. Both pieces of wisdom will help you live a healthier life.

Jesus' conversation with the disciples, in private, about the Pharisee's complaints regarding at least some of the disciple's table manners provided an opportunity for some additional teaching, and He gets their attention with a question that I think would hurt my feelings:

Are you so dull? Don't you see that nothing that enters a person from the outside can defile them?
Mark 7:18

In this teaching moment, He offers a foundational truth about our faith: it is not what we consume physically that defines us, but rather what resides in our hearts.

Jesus challenges the prevailing notions of purity and defilement, emphasizing that external actions and appearances are not what truly matter in our relationship with God. Instead, He points to the heart – the wellspring of our thoughts, intentions, and actions. This message is both liberating and convicting, calling us to reflect on the inner workings of our hearts.

In our culture, we often become preoccupied with outward appearances and societal expectations. Social media is rife with messages that bombard us from all sides. We may focus on adhering to rules or maintaining a certain image, thinking that this will earn us acceptance or righteousness. However, Jesus redirects our attention toward what is truly significant: the condition of our hearts. Are we harboring love, kindness, and forgiveness, or are we allowing bitterness, anger, and resentment to take root?

The call to examine our hearts prompts us to engage in self-reflection and spiritual growth. Just as gardeners tend to their plants, removing weeds and nourishing the soil, we too, must cultivate our hearts, allowing God's Word to guide and transform us. When we invite the Holy Spirit to work within us, we can begin to bear fruit that reflects Christ's love and character to the world around us.

LIVE UP: Are you attempting to cultivate an image for the acceptance of others rather than embracing the truth that you are a beloved child of God?

Let us welcome the truth that what truly matters to God is not our outward appearance but the state of our hearts. May we strive to align our inner lives with His will, allowing His grace to transform us from the inside out, so we can share His light with others.

Reading for Reflection: 1 Samuel 16:1-7; Luke 16:15

Appearances are often deceiving.
Aesop

◇◇◇

IN PROGRESS

Do you see anything?

Mark 8:23

Have you ever seen a photo of Ruth Graham's tombstone? I love her carefully selected epitaph:

End of Construction. Thank you for your patience!

She reminds us that we are all "Works in Progress," and that means there is more to be done. We do not yet see clearly or understand completely all that is going on in our world and in our own lives. In Mark, we read about Jesus healing a blind man in Bethsaida (see Mark 8:22-26). Scripture tells us, *"He (Jesus) took the blind man by the hand and led him outside the village. When he had spit on the man's eyes and put his hands on him, Jesus asked, 'Do you see anything?' "* This moment is significant, as it shows the intimate and personal nature of Jesus' healing ministry. While we don't know why Jesus did not heal everyone He encountered, His act of taking the blind man by the hand is a beautiful demonstration of His compassion and willingness to engage with those in need. By leading him away from the crowd, Jesus creates a space for personal connection and focused attention. This invites us to reflect on how God often desires to work in our lives – not in the chaos of the world, but in the quiet moments when we draw close to Him.

The method Jesus uses, spitting on the man's eyes, may seem unusual to us, but it emphasizes that healing can come in various forms. It reminds us that God's ways are not our own, and His methods can be surprising, and, in this moment, it feels a bit disgusting. In our lives, we may not always understand how God is working or the way He chooses to heal our wounds, whether physical, emotional, or spiritual.

When Jesus asks the blind man if he sees anything, it encourages us to examine our own spiritual sight. Are we open to seeing the work of God in our lives? Sometimes, our vision may be clouded by doubts, fears, or distractions. We need to bring these to Jesus, who can transform our perspective and help us see clearly.

LIVE UP: Is there an issue where I need clarity, a different perspective, or more focus to see how God wants to grow my trust and faith in Him and am I willing to live up to His call on my life?

Can we acknowledge our need for Jesus' touch in our lives? Can we seek His presence and guidance, trusting He knows the best ways to heal and restore us? In every encounter with Him, we can find hope, clarity, and renewed vision. Let us remember that in moments of uncertainty, Jesus is ready to lead us by the hand, guiding us into a deeper understanding of His love and purpose for our lives.

Reading for Reflection: Isaiah 53:1-6; Mark 11:24

Faith is taking the first step,
even when you don't see the whole staircase.
Martin Luther King Jr.

◇◇◇

ROAD LESS TRAVELED

*Which of these three do you think
was a neighbor to the man who fell into
the hands of robbers?*

Luke 10:36

We see this picture of a road, a path, and a way throughout the Old Testament. Then we come to the New Testament and the idea continues. Do you remember the story Jesus tells a lawyer and His own disciples in Luke 10? It was about a road, a bad road from Jerusalem to Jericho (see Luke 10:25-37). The road was dangerous, and it was on this road that a man was attacked, beaten, robbed, and left for dead. We know it as the story of the Good Samaritan. It was a story, like many of Jesus' stories that had a twist, a surprise. A priest passed by, and not only did he not help the man, but he also moved to the other side of the street. So did the Levite. The Samaritan was the least likely person to see the man and respond with care and compassion. But he recognized that what happened on the road was not all about him. He was traveling along a road, like you and me, with others.

Jesus had some more thoughts about roads too.

**But small is the gate and narrow the road
that leads to life, and only a few find it.
Matthew 7:14**

I am the way and the truth and the life.
No one comes to the Father except through me.
John 14:6

So, we are all on a journey, and we have two choices. We can take the Jesus Road, or we can take the Me Road. One involves sacrifice and surrender. The other invites us to a never-ending pursuit of self. But here's a reminder: whichever road you choose, there will be a host of decisions to make every single day.

LIVE UP: Which road will you choose?

There is a very popular message that dates back to a newspaper article written in 1914: *"It's not WHAT you know, but WHO you know."* The idea is that if you make it a practice to know the right people, then things will go better for you, you will have an advantage, and you will have a better chance at success. I would suggest that who you make the time to know is important, but the who may not be obvious. You might meet them on the road. We call these moments divine appointments.

Let us pray for open hearts that are sensitive to the needs of those around us. May we strive to be good neighbors, reflecting Christ's love in all our actions. In doing so, we fulfill the command to love our neighbors as ourselves, becoming agents of hope and healing in a world that desperately needs it.

Reading for Reflection: Isaiah 57:14-21; John 14:5-7

Do for ONE what you wish you could do for EVERYONE.
Andy Stanley

◇◇◇

WASH YOUR HANDS

*Did not the one who made the
outside make the inside also?*

Luke 11:40

Growing up I loved *Mr. Clean* commercials. It was the early days of television and a time when I still understood what the commercials were attempting to sell. Though I spent more time making messes than cleaning up, I was a *Mr. Clean* fan. The history of *Mr. Clean* commercials dates back to the brand's introduction in 1958 by Procter & Gamble. The character of *Mr. Clean*, a bald, muscular man dressed in a white t-shirt and pants, was created to embody cleanliness and efficiency in household cleaning. The original commercials featured *Mr. Clean* demonstrating the effectiveness of the cleaning product on various messy surfaces, promoting the idea that he could make any home spotless.

The Pharisee who hosted Jesus for a dinner party would have loved *Mr. Clean* but he was very disappointed in Jesus because He failed to wash his hands before the meal. (His mother, Mary, might have been disappointed too!) But the occasion of the meal provided an opportunity for another conversation-starting question from Jesus. He wanted to highlight a critical truth about the difference between being clean and looking clean.

Jesus challenged the religious leaders who were focused on external appearances, emphasizing that God looks beyond the surface to the condition of our hearts. The Pharisees were meticulous about following the laws and traditions, ensuring their actions aligned with societal expectations. But their focus on outward appearances blinded them to the deeper issues of pride, hypocrisy, and a lack of genuine love for others. Jesus' words serve as a wake-up call, reminding us that external actions alone do not equate to righteousness. The inside-outside question invites us to examine our own lives.

LIVE UP: Am I too caught up in appearances, worried more about how I appear than honest about the purity of my thoughts and attitudes?

It is easy to present ourselves in a way that meets societal standards while neglecting the inner transformation that God desires. Jesus calls us to prioritize the heart – our thoughts, intentions, and relationships – with God and others. True purity comes from a heart surrendered to God. It is about allowing His grace to cleanse us from within, shaping our character and influencing our actions. When we seek to cultivate a heart that reflects His love, we become vessels of His grace in the world, demonstrating authenticity and humility.

May God help us focus less on outward appearances and more on the condition of our hearts. May we seek His transformation from the inside out, allowing His Spirit to work within us. In doing so, we can live authentically, reflecting His light and love to those around us.

Reading for Reflection: Psalms 86:11; Luke 6:43-45

As for reputation, though it be a glorious instrument
of advancing our Master's service, yet there is a better than that:
a clean heart, a single eye, and a soul full of God. A fair exchange if,
by the loss of reputation, we can purchase the lowest
degree of purity of heart.
John Wesley

◇◇◇

BOLD PRAYERS

However, when the Son of Man comes,
will he find faith on the earth?

Luke 18:8

I love stories, hearing them, reading them, telling them, and that makes the parables of Jesus some of my very favorite portions of Scripture. The parable Jesus tells of a widow relentlessly seeking justice from an unjust judge is special to me and one of the most complicated, in my opinion, to unpack. Persistence in prayer, justice for the oppressed, and faith on earth are all elements Jesus includes in very few words (see Luke 18:1-8).

The widow's relentless persistence, even in the face of indifference, exemplifies a tenacious faith that refuses to give up, and it reminds me of a widow in the church where I grew up. Though I never knew much of her story, I experienced first-hand her generous spirit, positive testimony, and faithfulness in prayer. Velma was a blessing to me and anyone who crossed her path. Her faith was contagious, and she never left you wondering about the source of her tenacity and hope. When I read the story Jesus tells in Luke 18, Velma's face is in my mind.

The question Jesus asks at the conclusion of this parable reminds us that true faith is not passive acceptance or fleeting emotion, but an active, persistent pursuit of God, even amidst adversity and unanswered prayers. It's a faith that endures, but it also highlights the inherent challenge of maintaining faith in a world often characterized by suffering, injustice, and unanswered prayers. The parable showcases the difficulty the widow faces, symbolizing the struggles we as believers experience on our faith journey.

Jesus' question isn't merely rhetorical; it serves as a call to action. It challenges us to examine our own faith, to cultivate perseverance in prayer, and to actively demonstrate our belief in God through their actions. But there is such good news in this story because the widow's perseverance is rewarded in the parable. This underscores the importance of persistence in prayer. God may not always answer our prayers in the way or the time we expect, but unwavering faith, persistent seeking, and continued prayer demonstrate trust in God's character and timing.

LIVE UP: Do I have some doubts I am dealing with right now or have I given up praying for a problem or a person or a problem person somewhere along the way because I lost hope? Can I begin again to pray with persistence, confident that God hears my prayers and is always at work on both ends of every situation?

Jesus offers each of us a powerful call to deepen our faith and to live out our beliefs with unwavering commitment, like the persistent widow. May we approach God with confidence, knowing that He hears our cries and will ultimately provide justice and resolution. Let us not grow weary in our seeking but continue to trust in His goodness and faithfulness, even when we don't immediately see the answers to our prayers. In our persistence, we discover a deeper faith and a closer relationship with our loving and just Heavenly Father.

Reading for Reflection: 2 Chronicles 6:20; Hebrews 4:14-16

Bold prayers honor God, and God honors bold prayers.
Mark Batterson

◇◇◇

SPEAK UP

Speak up for those who cannot speak for themselves, for the rights of all who are destitute. Speak up and judge fairly; defend the rights of the poor and needy.

Proverbs 31:8-9

Follow Close - John 1:38

A Testimony - John 5:44

Quitting - John 6:67

Yes, Lord Yes - Matthew 9:28

Hide and Go Seek - Luke 15:4

A Failure to Say Thanks - Luke 17:17

Know Your Audience - Matthew 21:31

Lineage and Legacy - Matthew 22:42

Purpose Driven - Matthew 26:54

◇◇◇

FOLLOW CLOSE

What do you want?

John 1:38

An unexpected email connected me with a young man who I had not seen in over 30 years. The reunion began when his mom gifted Brit with a box of memorabilia from his teenage years. Brit discovered a magazine article and some photographs of the two of us which led him to try and figure out if I was still alive and what I might be doing these days. A quick internet search located me, and it was fun to reconnect electronically and a few weeks later for lunch. What I loved most was learning that he had pursued a call to pastoral ministry that he had articulated as a 15-year-old and was currently serving a church in San Antonio. His story surprised me because I did not realize that his call to ministry came beside a pond while we were fishing at a summer youth camp. Though I did not remember responding to a question he asked about God's call on my life, he told me that it was in that moment he realized God was calling him. Though the road was not straight, he answered the call and followed Jesus and is joyfully serving as a shepherd to a wonderful congregation.

John the Baptist, having identified Jesus as the Lamb of God, directed two of his disciples to physically follow Jesus (see John 1:35-42). While walking, Jesus turns and asks them a very simple question wanting to know what it is that they want. The two disciples, Andrew, and an unnamed companion, had been following John the Baptist, seeking spiritual fulfillment and guidance. Their willingness to leave John and follow Jesus demonstrates an openness to new possibilities and a desire for deeper truth. Their response to Jesus' call reflects a faith that is both courageous and humble.

I love the question Jesus asked: *"What do you want?"* and I believe it is one that He is still asking. It is more than a casual inquiry; it's an invitation to self-reflection. He invited the two disciples to examine their motivations, to clarify their intentions, and to understand the commitment they were making. And the question challenges each of us to consider what truly drives our faith.

The disciples' subsequent actions reveal the depth of their commitment. Andrew, after discovering the identity of Jesus, immediately seeks out his brother Simon Peter, sharing the good news and leading Peter to encounter Jesus. This act of evangelism demonstrates a commitment to sharing the transformative power of faith with others. It suggests that true discipleship involves not only a personal commitment to Christ but also a willingness to share His message with the world.

SPEAK UP: Am I seeking spiritual fulfillment, personal gain, social acceptance, or something else? Is God talking to me about a deeper commitment, a special ministry, a new assignment of service? Do I know God's dream for my future?

Following Jesus' call has taken me to places and connected me with people I could never have dreamed possible, people like Brit. I'm living proof of God's promise through the Apostle Paul in Ephesians 3:20 for Him to do more than I could ever imagine. Jesus' question encourages us to examine the depths of our hearts and to ensure that our pursuit of faith is rooted in a sincere desire to follow Him and to live according to His teachings.

May we be inspired by the disciples' willingness to leave behind familiar comforts and follow Jesus' call. Let's be ready to share the good news with others, reflecting Christ's love everywhere He leads.

Reading for Reflection: Jonah 2:1-10; Hebrews 12:1-2

We are never short on opportunities to answer the call
to assist the widows, support the homeless, stand up for justice
and to preach Christ crucified and resurrected.
That is the true calling of every believer.
Andrena Sawyer

◇◇◇

A TESTIMONY

*How can you believe since you accept
glory from one another but do not seek the
glory that comes from the only God?*

John 5:44

One of my very favorite Tony Campolo stories, and there are many, happened in his local church where his pastor began a Sunday morning sermon focused on graduates who were sitting on the front row dressed in their academic regalia. His opening words as I recall, were these:

Children, you are going to die!
And after you die, you will be buried in the ground.
Dirt will be thrown on your casket.
The people will then return to the church and
eat potato salad and talk about you.
And on that day the question will not be,
did you have a title, the question will be,
did you have a testimony?

A title? What you had accomplished. A testimony? What you were known for. Powerful questions in my opinion and though I heard them for the first time almost a half-century ago, they remain with me today.

Jesus poses a challenging question to the Jewish leaders in John 5. Delivered amidst a powerful discourse on faith and the identity of Jesus, He spoke directly to the human desire for recognition and the importance of seeking true honor (see John 5:31-47). The Jewish leaders, deeply entrenched in their societal structures and traditions, sought validation and approval from their peers. This human inclination towards seeking honor from others is a common struggle. We often find ourselves seeking affirmation from our colleagues, friends, or family members. We desire recognition for our achievements and accomplishments, believing it will bring us fulfillment and a sense of worth.

The words of Jesus challenge this perspective. He points to a higher source of honor – the glory that comes from God alone. True honor comes not from human accolades but from living a life aligned with God's will and reflecting His character in our words and actions. This kind of honor is not dependent on external approval; it is an intrinsic reward that stems from a deep relationship with God. Jesus' question compels us to examine the motivations behind our actions. Are we driven by a desire for human approval, or is our focus on pleasing God? When we seek honor from others, we risk building our lives on an unstable foundation. True fulfillment and lasting satisfaction are found only in seeking the glory that comes from God.

SPEAK UP: What is more important, my achievements or my investment in others? When my life is over, will my testimony be what my family and friends talk about? Whose life is being positively impacted because of my service on their behalf?

Here are a few more clarifying questions: Where do we seek our validation? Are we seeking human praise or divine approval? May we choose to align our lives with God's will, allowing our actions to reflect His character. This may involve challenging our desires for human recognition and instead focusing on what pleases Him. In seeking God's glory, we find true and lasting honor, a sense of purpose that transcends the temporary and brings fulfillment to our lives.

Reading for Reflection: Isaiah 6:1-10; John 4:39

Jesus teaches us another way: Go out. Go out and share your testimony, go out and interact with your brothers, go out and share, go out and ask. Become the Word in body as well as spirit.
Pope Francis

◇◇◇

QUITTING

You do not want to leave too, do you?

John 6:67

One of the most meaningful and painful conversations that I ever had with my mother came during my high school years. I had given up a part in a musical because I didn't get the part for which I had auditioned. Looking back now it seems especially funny because I am not blessed with a great singing voice, so it is amazing that the director had even gifted me with a part! My mother didn't care about the part in the musical, but what she did care about was my attitude, my response to disappointment, and my propensity to quit something if I didn't get my way. She made her point in our conversation. I was hurt, and I determined in those uncomfortable moments that I didn't want to be known as a quitter. I would do better in the future and hopefully, I have.

Jesus asks what feels like a distressing question after many of His followers have turned away due to the high standard His teachings presented (see John 6:60-70). Followers were fading and Jesus had a heart-to-heart conversation with His 12 disciples. His question invites a moment of reflection. It's a call to examine our own commitment to Him, especially during difficult times. Just as the disciples were confronted with a decision, we too, encounter moments in our faith journey that challenge our resolve and understanding. When faced with trials, doubts, or cultural pressures, it can be tempting to walk away, to seek comfort in what feels easier or more palatable.

I love Peter's response: *"Lord, to whom shall we go? You have the words of eternal life."* While Peter often gives us a chance to criticize his impulsiveness, his response in this moment captures the heart of a true disciple. It acknowledges that while the path may be difficult, Jesus is the source of life and truth. In our own lives, we are called to recognize that no alternative holds the promise of eternal fulfillment apart from Christ.

In moments of uncertainty, we must remember that walking away from Jesus means walking away from the only One who can provide true peace, purpose, and direction. Instead of retreating when our faith is tested, we can lean into our relationship with Him, seeking understanding through prayer, scripture, and community.

SPEAK UP: Are there areas in my life where I feel tempted to turn away?

Jesus invites us to stay, to engage, and to trust in His promises. Perhaps this is a moment to hold on, hang tight, kneel down, and ask God for a fresh anointing, an extra measure of grace, a verse we can claim as His voice speaking directly to us. May we choose to follow Him wholeheartedly, embracing the hope and eternal life He offers.

Reading for Reflection: Job 13:13-15; Colossians 4:2-6

Becoming a Christian is the work of a moment;
being a Christian is the work of a lifetime.
Billy Graham

◇◇◇

YES, LORD YES

Do you believe that I am able to do this?

Matthew 9:28

A very large window in my office provides a wonderful view of one of the quad spaces on our university campus. Over the years I've watched dogs chase frisbees, students play in the snow, our marching band practice, and even witnessed a marriage proposal or two. But my most powerful memory is watching a blind student navigate the campus with grace and confidence. Her ability to traverse sidewalks and stairs regardless of the weather never ceased to amaze me. My admiration for her grew each time I watched out my window.

Blindness is the context for Jesus' question as He encounters two sightless men seeking mercy (see Matthew 9:27-34). Their response is powerful – they affirm their faith in answering His question by saying, *"Yes, Lord."* This moment is a beautiful illustration of the connection between faith and the miraculous work of Jesus. The blind men's persistence in seeking Jesus shows us the importance of pursuing Him with unwavering faith. Despite their physical limitations and societal challenges, they refuse to be deterred. They recognize Jesus as the Messiah, the Son of David, and they come to Him with their need, demonstrating a faith that is both humble and bold.

Jesus' question, *"Do you believe that I am able to do this?"* is not merely a formality; it serves as an invitation for the men to express their faith. Our belief in Jesus' power to transform our circumstances is crucial. He often asks us to articulate our faith, not for His benefit, but for ours – to strengthen our trust in Him. When the blind men testify to their belief,

Jesus responds with compassion and action. He touches their eyes and says, *"According to your faith let it be done to you."* In this moment, their faith is rewarded, and they receive their sight. This powerful encounter reminds us that Jesus is always willing to meet us in our need, but our faith is a key component in receiving His grace and healing.

SPEAK UP: What am I in need of today? Will I pray specifically with faith for God to answer my request?

I love the little chorus, *Yes, Lord Yes,* and its roots are in the contemporary Christian music movement of the late 20th century. The chorus emphasizes a posture of obedience and surrender to God, reflecting the believer's desire to respond affirmatively to God's calling. The lyrics express a commitment to follow God's will, encapsulating the essence of faith and submission to divine guidance. As we walk through this day, may we approach God with the same boldness as the blind men, trusting in His ability to work miracles in our lives. In every situation, let us declare, *"Yes, Lord Yes,"* and watch as He moves in response to our faith.

Reading for Reflection: Psalms 77; Acts 9:10-18

> *God gives His power for His purposes. He doesn't give*
> *you His power for your purposes. He doesn't expect you to*
> *fulfill His purposes in your power. His power for His purposes.*
> **Kevin Myers**

◇◇◇

HIDE AND GO SEEK

*Suppose one of you has a hundred
sheep and loses one of them. Doesn't he
leave the ninety-nine in the open
country and go after the lost sheep
until he finds it?*

Luke 15:4

Historians trace the game of *Hide and Go Seek* to ancient civilizations, first mentioned in the works of the Roman author Ovid, born in 43 BC. But an argument can be made that the first record of this game was in the Garden of Eden, though there was nothing fun about what was going on when God sought Adam for a critical conversation about sin. The third chapter of Genesis is filled with questions and all the participants (God, Adam, Eve, and Satan) take their turn posing inquiries of each other.

Jesus chooses the metaphor of sheep to ask an important question about our responsibility to one another. Lost sheep, and lost people matter, they are important, and they require immediate attention. Search parties need to be organized and sent out with no time to waste. Here is what is most interesting to me, God knows where lost sheep and lost people are located and He does not need the help of the Global Positioning System (GPS).

GPS would not be invented until the 1950s, but God's Positioning System has been working since creation, and He did not need to ask

Adam the question about his location nor did He ever wonder about where the prodigal had wandered. But God asked Adam (*"Where are you?" Genesis 3:9*) and He continues to ask prodigals. I call that grace with a good measure of accountability. While He does not have to communicate with us, He chooses to, and He loves it when we talk to Him.

The fact that God asks questions says a great deal about our relationship. Clear guidelines were set in the beginning, and He loves us so much that He wants to hold us accountable and He is always willing to talk to us, even when, maybe especially when, we fail. Adam experienced the gift of a Heavenly Father on that day in the garden; not only was He the creator, He was the redeemer. And He still is.

Growing up I loved the game of Hide and Go Seek, but if I got my choice, I wanted to be the one to hide. While I loved finding a great place to hide, I discovered early it was not much fun to stay hidden. I wanted to be found. The game is timeless. I've played it with my kids and now my grandkids, and over the years, I've discovered that some of us want to be found more than others. My youngest granddaughter will announce where she is even before you find her. While it kind of defeats the purpose of the game, I love that she wants me to find her. And her actions remind me that deep down, we all want to be found, even when we don't act like it.

SPEAK UP: Are you hiding from God?

God knows exactly where you are today and if Scripture and experience teach us anything, He is relentless and patient in His loving pursuit. Amazingly, this truth applies to every single person on the planet. As you cross paths with many or only a few this day, be reminded that you might be a part of their search and rescue party.

Reading for Reflection: Psalms 139; John 10:25-30

Jesus leaving the 99 to find 1 seems crazy until you are that 1.
Toby Mac

◇◇◇

A FAILURE TO SAY THANKS

Where are the other nine?

Luke 17:17

Ten lepers stood at a distance from Jesus and asked him to take pity on their condition (see Luke 17:11-19). Jesus gave them instructions to go and make an appearance before the priests. No instant healing, no message of encouragement, instead some simple instructions. Scripture tells us that *"as they went,"* they were healed. The power and creativity of Jesus were once again on display and at this point in the gospels, his ability to heal was no longer a surprise.

The shocking moment comes a short time later when we learn that only one of the ten returns to say thank you by throwing himself at the feet of Jesus, *"and he was a Samaritan."*

Ten percent, only one out of ten, says thank you. Sad, but it seems about right when we begin to reflect on how seldom we hear these words which were some of the first our parents tried to teach us: thank you.

Spending time with grateful people always encourages me. Years ago, I met a man who did real estate appraisal work. Our phone conversation convinced me that he was the person to hire for a special project and when it was completed, we met in an attorney's office for him to share the results. I liked him even more in person than I did over the phone. He exuded gratitude in his words and his actions. The business relationship led to a friendship that included some great moments on the golf course and flying aerobatics in his 1941 Stearman biplane.

Trust me when I tell you that I was so grateful to be back safely on solid ground after barrel rolls and a hammerhead done on that flight!

My friend offered grace to everyone who crossed his path, and each time I left his presence, I wanted to be more like him. He would have been the one who returned to Jesus and gave thanks. Far too often, I have been one of the nine.

These days, I am trying to give thanks in every circumstance, say thank you more often (in person, via texts, emails, and in letters), and surprise people (some who I have not seen or spoken with in years) with expressions of my gratitude for their investment in my life.

SPEAK UP: What if all I had today was what I thanked the Lord for yesterday?

I felt convicted when I heard someone ask this question. Some days, I would have very little, for I've failed to express my gratitude for God's blessings. Let's up the percentage of thankful people and give thanks with a grateful heart. I know we can do better than 10 percent!

Reading for Reflection: Psalms 100; 2 Corinthians 9:10-15

Gratitude is the healthiest of all human emotions.
The more you express gratitude for what you have, the more
likely you will have even more to express gratitude for.
Zig Ziglar

◇◇◇

KNOW YOUR AUDIENCE

*Which of the two did
what his father wanted?*

Matthew 21:31

Any experienced speaker will stress the importance of knowing your audience in advance of preparing and then delivering a message. On more than one occasion, I have finished speaking and realized that I had not done enough research or asked enough questions about who would be present to hear my message, and that's never a good feeling.

Jesus, being omniscient, always knew His audience, and perhaps that is what makes the questions He asked throughout the Gospels so brilliant. In Matthew 21, Jesus enters the Temple and engages with the chief priests and elders who were steeped in Jewish tradition (see Matthew 21:23-46). His interchange with a mixture of enlightening and convicting parables is fascinating. Jesus knew His audience.

The lesser-known parable about two sons sets the stage for Jesus' question to the religious leaders. One son - initially refuses to work in his father's vineyard but later repents and obeys, while the other initially agrees but ultimately disobeys. He uses this parable to expose the hypocrisy of the religious leaders and to emphasize the importance of genuine obedience over outward conformity. The parable highlights the contrast between outward obedience and inward rebellion. The first son, while initially disobedient, ultimately repents and does his father's will. The second son, however, outwardly agrees to work in the vineyard but fails to follow through. The parable paints a sad picture of the religious leaders, who outwardly adhered to the law but inwardly rejected God's message.

Jesus' question, *"Which of the two did what his father wanted?"* is not merely rhetorical; it's a direct challenge to their self-righteousness. They were quick to judge and condemn others while neglecting their own obedience to God. The parable serves as a powerful reminder that true faith is not about outward conformity but about an inward transformation of the heart.

SPEAK UP: Am I guilty of a double life, where things look good on the outside, but the shadow side is alive and well and dragging me down? Do my words match my actions and do my actions match what is going on in my heart and mind?

This parable invites us to reflect on our own lives and our relationship with God. Are we outwardly religious, attending services and engaging in a small group, yet failing to fully obey His commandments? Or are we genuinely seeking to align our hearts and actions with His will? True obedience goes beyond simply following rules; it involves a commitment to transforming our hearts and allowing God's love to guide our lives. Jesus' question also encourages us to be honest about our own shortcomings. Just as the first son eventually repented and obeyed his father, we, too, have the opportunity to turn from our disobedience and seek a closer relationship with God. It is through repentance and a commitment to follow Him that we experience true freedom and spiritual growth.

Reading for Reflection: Deuteronomy 30:16; 2 Corinthians 10:5-7

Obedience to God's will is the secret of spiritual knowledge and insight. It is not willingness to know, but willingness to do (obey) God's will that brings certainty.
Eric Liddell

◇◇◇

LINEAGE AND LEGACY

What do you think about the Messiah?
Whose son is he?

Matthew 22:42

One of my extended family members decided to explore the history of our family and he passed along an electronic file filled with newspaper articles, certificates of birth and death, obituaries, census records, and a host of other interesting material. His work prompted another family member to subscribe to Ancestry.com, a company with a massive collection of digitized electronic records. As I reviewed the work produced by my family members, I caught the bug and began to do my own research. Why is it that we are so fascinated about the past and discovering whether or not we might be related to a Civil War soldier or one of the authors of the Declaration of Independence? Our heritage certainly helps shape us, but every single one of us chooses the decisions we will make and the legacy we will leave for future generations.

The birth lineage of Jesus was of great interest to at least two of the Gospel writers and for different reasons. Matthew writing to a primarily Jewish audience traces Jesus back to Abraham, the man considered the Father of the Jewish nation. The physician Luke, a Gentile, goes back farther, in fact, all the way back to Adam because he wanted to share the message that Jesus was the Savior of all, not just the Jewish nation.

Jesus engages in a fascinating conversation with the scribes in Matthew's Gospel (see Matthew 22:41-45), and he poses a series of challenging questions regarding His identity and authority, something that they were questioning. The questions were designed to provoke thought, challenge assumptions, and unveil the truth about His identity. Jesus, the Messiah, should not have been a surprise as His birth, life, death, and resurrection were foretold and known by Jews, especially their religious leaders. His question went right to the very heart of Jewish expectation and belief. The Messiah was widely anticipated, yet there were varying interpretations of His lineage and role. Jesus' question forces them to confront their preconceived notions and acknowledge the complexities of messianic prophecy. Their answer – that Christ was the son of David – sets the stage for more questions.

I love that Jesus quotes Scripture, Psalms 110:1, in this interaction with the scribes. King David in this psalm highlights the inherent tension between his lineage and the Messiah's divine authority. David, a human king, calls the Messiah "Lord," indicating a higher authority. This underscores the Messiah's divine nature and his role as both a descendant of David and the Son of God. The Pharisees, caught in their literal interpretations, fail to grasp the deeper meaning of Scripture.

SPEAK UP: Am I hiding God's Word in my heart? Am I disciplined in my study of Scripture seeking to see God's plan and hear His voice as He directs my paths? How might my life change if I increased the time spent with Him?

Jesus reminds us that He is both the descendant of David, fulfilling prophecy, and the Son of God, possessing ultimate authority. May we be willing to challenge our preconceived notions and allow God's Word to transform our understanding. Just as Jesus challenged the Pharisees, may we be challenged to critically examine our own beliefs and approach our faith with humility and openness. Get into the Word and let the Word get into you.

Reading for Reflection: Isaiah 7:14; Revelation 1:1-3

God is the one who satisfies the passion for justice,
the longing for spirituality, the hunger for relationship,
the yearning for beauty. And God, the true God, is the God we see in
Jesus of Nazareth, Israel's Messiah, the world's true Lord.
N.T. Wright

◇◇◇

PURPOSE DRIVEN

But how then would the Scriptures
be fulfilled that say it must
happen in this way?

Matthew 26:54

Pastor Rick Warren wrote a best-selling book a few years back, *The Purpose Driven Life.* The book guides readers on a spiritual journey to discover their God-given purpose through a 40-day program. It highlights five key purposes: worship, ministry, evangelism, fellowship, and discipleship. The program encourages individuals to live a life centered on serving God and others. I loved the book and I'm a big fan of finding your purpose and living into it, but what I've discovered over the years is the reality of circumstances challenging or, in some cases, wrecking our plans to live life with purpose.

Jesus asks an important question to Peter during His arrest in the Garden (see Matthew 26:47-56). In the moment, God's plan was unfolding in a way the disciples did not expect and through circumstances that seemed confusing and painful. At this point in the narrative, Jesus is fully aware of the impending suffering He will face. Despite the chaos around Him – the betrayal, the arrest, and the impending crucifixion – He remains calm and resolute. His question highlights the importance of fulfilling Scripture and reveals that every event is part of a greater divine purpose, even those that seem unjust.

Most mornings I take a few minutes to catch up on the news from overnight. Seldom do I not read a story that breaks my heart, creates a need to pray, and leaves me with a question or two about how God will work in the midst of this tragedy and suffering. But I believe with all my heart that God has a plan, and He is in the middle of every difficult situation that challenges our faith. We might be tempted to react impulsively, like Peter. We might struggle to see how our struggles fit into God's greater narrative. However, just as Jesus reassured His disciples, we are reminded that God's sovereignty encompasses all things, including our trials.

I am also reminded of Jesus' willingness to submit to God's plan, even at great personal cost, modeling for us the strength found in obedience. We can find peace amid turmoil when we trust in God's purposes. It encourages us to embrace a posture of faith, surrendering our desires and expectations to Him.

SPEAK UP: Are circumstances or events challenging my faith, and am I spending my time worrying, questioning, or giving them to God in faith that His purpose will prevail?

"Keep short accounts with God," I heard those words in sermons often growing up. Great advice for staying connected with our Heavenly Father and remembering that He is at work in our lives, even when we cannot see it. May we trust that His plans are perfect and that He uses every circumstance for our growth and His glory. In our moments of doubt or confusion, let us seek to align our hearts with His will, knowing that He is the author of our story.

Reading for Reflection: Isaiah 41:10; Romans 10:5-13

God did not call us to be successful. He called us to be faithful.
Mother Teresa

◇◇◇

TAKE UP

Then he said to them all: "Whoever wants to be my disciple must deny themselves and take up their cross daily and follow me."

Matthew 16:24

Leap of Faith - John 3:12

Rock the Boat - Matthew 8:26

Big Ears - John 8:43

Proud Hearts and Dirty Feet - John 13:12

Test Questions - Matthew 21:25

Break a Vase - Matthew 26:10

Hurry, Please! - Luke 18:41

Rising Doubts - Luke 24:38

Fixer Upper - John 21:22

◇◇◇

LEAP OF FAITH

I have spoken to you of earthly things
and you do not believe; how then will you
believe if I speak of heavenly things?

John 3:12

Bruce was my partner. I was 19 years of age. It was my first shift as a newly minted Houston Police Officer. We were assigned to one of the higher crime areas of the city. Before we had completed loading our cruiser with notepads, flashlights, and a shotgun, the dispatcher called our unit number and directed us to respond to a prowler reported by a frightened resident. I still remember the ride to the address provided to us via the police radio. Though I had been trained, tested, and now commissioned, I was scared, nauseous, and fairly certain that I might be sick - not a great way to start my new career! I survived the first call and then the second, returned to work the next night and eventually became a seasoned law enforcement professional. But in the beginning, it was new, my confidence was low, and my anxiety was high. I needed my faith to grow and over time, it did.

Jesus met a man who chose to visit him at night (John 3:1-15). His name was Nicodemus, a respected Pharisee whose confidence appeared to be low and his anxiety high. Though a religious leader, he struggled to understand what Jesus was teaching. Still, he was intrigued, curious, and eager to learn about this one who spoke of eternal life and the necessity of faith. Nicodemus struggled to grasp this concept of being "born again," but Jesus' response highlights a fundamental principle:

belief in earthly, observable truths helps one understand and accept heavenly, spiritual realities. These truths are a foundation for the leap of faith.

Nicodemus, like many of us today, may have been more comfortable with the tangible, the observable, the readily explainable, but saving faith requires a leap to a whole new level. We are invited to believe in heavenly things – the promises of eternal life, the forgiveness of sins, and the presence of God's kingdom. Jesus' question was not intended to discourage or dismiss those struggling with faith. Instead, it's a call to cultivate a deeper understanding of belief. It's a reminder that our faith journey involves a process of growth and transformation, beginning with acknowledging the evidence of God's presence in our lives. This might involve reflecting on moments of answered prayer, experiences of God's comfort, or witnessing His grace in others' lives.

TAKE UP: Have I taken the time to acknowledge the evidence of God's presence and power in my own life? Am I grounded in the promises and power of His Word? Will I walk by faith, not by sight?

Study the life of Nicodemus, and you will find a person who experienced a growing faith and clarity gained by spending time with others who believed. It led him to join Joseph of Arimathea in burying the body of Jesus in the tomb after the crucifixion. The life of Nicodemus reminds me that progressive faith is a faith to be celebrated. Let's commit to helping those who need a little patience before they leap. It will be worth the wait.

Reading for Reflection: Proverbs 14:15; Romans 14:1-9

Making a leap into the unknown is always terrifying.
But you know what's even scarier? Letting fear rob you
of God's amazing possibilities.
Unknown

◇◇◇

ROCK THE BOAT

You of little faith, why are you so afraid?

Matthew 8:26

A winter fishing trip to a "heat lake" in northwest Arkansas created some of the scariest moments of my life. A heat lake experiences elevated temperatures due to the water helping produce electricity. Fishermen love heat lakes because the fish grow faster and larger. Three of us found ourselves fishing on this lake with an 85-degree water temperature when a cold front arrived at 3:00 am, bringing sleet, snow, and powerful gusts of wind. We made a run for the primitive boat ramp where we had launched, and our captain donned a motorcycle helmet as protection from the weather in an attempt to steer the boat to safety. Though I had dodged a few bullets as a police officer, the fear from this fishing trip left me cold and shaking.

The question from Jesus unfolds after He is awakened while sleeping peacefully on a boat with His disciples (see Matthew 8:23-27). These seasoned fishermen, accustomed to the unpredictable nature of the sea, were convinced that they were about to drown. In the face of a fierce storm, their fear overwhelmed them, and they cried out to Jesus for help.

Can you relate? I confess to praying in a boat and many other situations that felt chaotic, frightening, and out of my control. While we may have faith - when the storms of life rage around us – be it financial struggles, health issues, or relational tensions – our fear can cloud our trust in God. Jesus' question, *"Why are you so afraid?"* challenges us to examine our own hearts. It's a call to reflect on our faith in Him. Do we truly believe that He is with us in our storms? Jesus did not promise us a life free from challenges, but He assured us of His presence and power in the midst of them.

TAKE UP: Is there an issue, a relationship, or a challenge I am currently facing that has me afraid and feeling more than a little helpless?

When Jesus speaks to the winds and the waves, and they obey Him, it illustrates His authority over all creation. This same authority is available to us today. In our moments of fear, we can turn to Him, knowing that He is capable of calming the storms in our lives. Let us choose faith over fear. May we acknowledge our anxieties but not allow them to dictate our response. Instead, let us remember that we are never alone; Jesus is with us, ready to bring peace into our tumultuous circumstances. Embrace the truth that in every storm, we can find refuge in Him.

Reading for Reflection: Psalms 107:29; Matthew 7:24-27

When the storms of life come, if they come to
me personally, to my family or to the world,
I want to be strong enough to stand and be a strength
to somebody else, be shelter for somebody else.
Anne Graham Lotz

◇◇◇

BIG EARS

Why is my language not clear to you?

John 8:43

Multitaskers are terrible listeners. Trust me, I know because I counted multitasking as some sort of unnamed spiritual gift. But the ability to check lots of "to do" boxes in record time creates a whole different set of challenges, often ones for which we are unaware. If someone had asked me if I was a good listener, I would have argued that I was, but I was kidding myself and disrespecting others, somehow believing that my time was more valuable than theirs.

Jesus asked an important question to His crowd of Jewish followers (see John 8:42-47) and then provided an immediate answer, *"Because you are unable to hear what I say."* This statement underscores a crucial truth about communication and understanding – particularly in our relationship with God. Jesus is speaking to those who are resistant to His message, highlighting the barriers that can prevent us from truly hearing and understanding His words.

At its core, this verse challenges us to examine our own hearts and minds. Are we genuinely receptive to the truth that God speaks into our lives? Often, we may find ourselves preoccupied with distractions, doubts, or preconceived notions that cloud our ability to listen. Just as the religious leaders struggled to comprehend Jesus' message, we too can allow our biases and distractions to hinder our spiritual growth.

Listening is an act of humility and openness. It requires us to set aside our own agendas and be willing to engage with the truth, even when it challenges us. Jesus invites us to approach Him with a posture of curiosity and receptivity, longing to hear His voice above the noise of the world around us. Additionally, this verse reminds us of the importance of discernment. Not every voice we hear is aligned with God's truth. We must cultivate an ability to discern what is from Him and what is not. This involves spending time in prayer, studying Scripture, and seeking the guidance of the Holy Spirit.

TAKE UP: When was the last time I heard the voice of God?

Could we commit to becoming better listeners – both to God and to one another? Let us create space in our lives for His truth to penetrate our hearts, transforming our understanding and guiding our actions. In a world full of noise, may we strive to hear His voice clearly, leading us into a deeper relationship with Him and a greater understanding of His purpose for our lives. He's listening…are you?

Reading for Reflection: 1 Samuel 3:1-11; Luke 6:27

If you make listening and observation your occupation
you will gain much more than you can by talk.
Robert Baden-Powell

◇◇◇

PROUD HEARTS AND DIRTY FEET

When He had finished washing
their feet, He put on His clothes
and returned to His place.
Do you understand what
I have done for you?

John 13:12

What would you do if you had one week to live? Pause for a moment. Read the question again. Reflect on what you might choose to do. In the 13th chapter of John, we see how Jesus answered that question. As time was counting down Jesus did not go out and preach to great crowds, heal the sick, or raise the dead. Instead, He chose to hang out with friends…and wash their dirty feet (see John 13:1-17).

I don't know how you feel about feet, but I confess they are one of my least favorite subjects. Feet are an important part of life, but I see them as kind of personal so I'm glad that I live in a time of socks and shoes and automobiles. Years ago, Dr. Scholl's had a television commercial for foot powder. It featured a dog bringing his master the evening newspaper. The man is seated in his recliner and the dog is standing erect on his back legs with the paper in his mouth. The man kicked off his shoes and the dog passed out. I loved that commercial!

These friends of Jesus had walked through the dirty roads of Palestine to get to the upper room. We assume they wore the open sandals of the day so their feet must have been smelly and dirty. The usual custom of the home was to provide a servant to wash the feet of the guests, but apparently, someone dropped the ball.

Think about it; who was the least likely person in the room to wash feet? If you answered Jesus, I think you would be correct. But Jesus once again demonstrates live last leadership. He does what no one else wants to do. His hands, which would soon be pierced, got dirty when He went to work washing feet.

TAKE UP: Am I willing to do the good work today that Jesus has prepared in advance for me to do (Ephesians 2:10) regardless of how challenging, anonymous, or inconveniencing it may be?

While the cleanliness of the disciple's feet was important, I believe it was the condition of their heart (and ours) that Jesus was most interested in. Let's follow the example of our leader, humble ourselves, and look for someone to serve. When we serve, we *understand* exactly what Jesus did for His disciples with a towel and a basin.

Reading for Reflection: Proverbs 11:2; James 3:13-18

Pride makes us artificial and humility makes us real.
Thomas Merton

◇◇◇

TEST QUESTIONS

*John's baptism – where did it
come from? Was it from heaven,
or of human origin?*

Matthew 21:25

As a nineteen-year-old, I took an oath and was commissioned as a law enforcement officer with all the tools of the trade, uniform, badge, handcuffs, and gun, but all of the equipment paled compared to the authority entrusted to me. At the time I was too young and inexperienced to recognize the significance of what had happened on that Friday night. Authority was a concept that I understood but never really considered. It became much clearer to me as I began to offer suspects their Miranda warnings, place them in handcuffs, and take away their freedom through incarceration. I learned quickly that this kind of authority was a big deal.

The religious leaders of Jesus' day recognized the importance of their authority, and after Jesus had cleansed the temple, the chief priest and elders questioned His authority (see Matthew 21:23-27). The experience led to a series of pointed questions that revealed the nature of Jesus' authority and the hypocrisy of his opponents. Jesus' response underscores the importance of discerning true authority and the dangers of rejecting divine truth.

The religious leaders, challenged by Jesus' actions, demand to know, *"By what authority are you doing these things? Who gave you this authority?"* These questions were not simply a request for credentials; they were a challenge to Jesus' legitimacy and a not-so-veiled attempt to discredit His ministry. They sought to undermine His authority by questioning its source. They were accustomed to a system of religious authority that was rooted in tradition and hierarchical structures, and Jesus' actions – particularly His clearing of the temple – disrupted that established order.

Jesus' response was so strategic. He didn't directly answer their question but instead posed a counter-question about John's baptism. The focus shifts from Jesus' authority to the authority of John the Baptist, whose ministry had already been recognized by many as divinely inspired. By challenging them to consider John's authority, Jesus indirectly establishes his own, as John had already identified Jesus as the Messiah. The religious leaders, caught in their own hypocrisy, are unable to answer Jesus' question. They recognize the divine origin of John's baptism but fear the consequences of acknowledging Jesus' authority. Their silence exposes their unwillingness to confront the truth and their commitment to maintaining their position of power. The encounter highlights the importance of discerning true authority for us all. True authority comes from God and is revealed through His Word.

TAKE UP: What guides my decisions and shapes my actions? Am I primarily influenced by the opinion of others, or do I trust in God's Word?

Let's be disciplined enough and patient enough to hear God's voice and seek His guidance. May we be willing to confront hypocrisy and embrace the truth, wherever it may lead. Let's pray for His will to be done on earth as it is in heaven. May we always remember that we serve under His authority as King of Kings and Lord of Lords. He has commissioned us to go and make disciples.

Reading for Reflection: Isaiah 5:16; Matthew 28:18-20

Nothing is impossible for the people of God who trust in the power of God to accomplish the will of God.
David Platt

◇◇◇

BREAK A VASE

Why are you bothering this woman?

Matthew 26:10

Students in my *New Testament Literature and Life* class may think I sound like a broken record because of the number of times they hear this message: **Context is King!** It is important, even imperative, when reading Scripture, but these days I'm discovering how critical it is in interpreting what we read or hear in the news, especially from those around us. You've said it or heard it said, *"If you only knew the whole story."* Well, the truth is that we seldom can have all the details, but gaining the context of a statement or action can certainly prevent us from misinterpreting or casting judgment, something we read in the story that leads Jesus to ask His disciples a pointed question.

This question arises in the context of the story of a woman anointing Jesus with expensive perfume (see Matthew 26:6-13). The disciples were angered, maybe even outraged, at what they perceived as a waste of valuable resources, but Jesus passionately defended the woman's actions. Anointing Jesus with perfume was an extravagant display of devotion, a costly offering, not for personal recognition or reward but as an expression of her heartfelt love and gratitude.

Giving, especially with extravagance, often brings criticism and judgment, maybe even some jealousy, as it did in this instance. The disciples were focused on the wrong thing. As they looked at the material value of the perfume, they failed to recognize the spiritual significance of the woman's actions. Jesus' question challenged them to examine their own responses to acts of faith and devotion. Their criticism highlighted the human tendency to judge others based on a limited perspective.

Like the disciples, we often fail to see the motivations behind others' actions, focusing on outward appearances rather than inner intentions. Jesus understood the woman's heart and commended her selfless act of love. He compares her selfless devotion with the impending betrayal He will face from one of His own disciples, and the contrast is dramatic.

TAKE UP: Have I been guilty of judging someone's words or actions without understanding the context? Am I giving with extravagance through my time, talent, and treasure? Who needs an investment, maybe an extravagant one, from me today?

May we learn to value selfless love and sacrifice, and may it be contagious. May we also examine our own hearts, ensuring that our actions are motivated by genuine faith and devotion, not mere outward conformity. Let Jesus' question continue to challenge us to see beyond the surface, to recognize the true worth of selfless love, and to motivate us to give in extravagant ways.

Reading for Reflection: Proverbs 21:26; 2 Corinthians 8:1-7

Since you cannot do good to all, you are to pay
special attention to those who, by the accident of time,
or place, or circumstances, are brought into
closer connection with you.
Saint Augustine

◇◇◇

HURRY PLEASE!

What do you want me to do for you?

Luke 18:41

Living in the present is not very easy sometimes, especially if the present is painful, or if we are waiting on something. I can remember being a young teenager in the early seventies. It was a time in the church where our choir sang *"The King is Coming."* It seemed like they sang it every Sunday. The most popular Christian books were about the Second Coming of Christ and it seemed like every Sunday School classroom had a chart in it that showed how everything was in line for Christ's imminent return. The pastor preached from Revelation on a regular basis, and I confess that I was not ready for Jesus to come and take us all to heaven. It was not a question of me not being a Christian, it was a question of me not having done all the things that I wanted to do in life.

I was living for the future. I was thinking about all of the real meaningful things in life that I had not yet had an opportunity to enjoy, like driving a car and kissing a girl, maybe even at the same time! Looking back now, that seems really immature, and I am sure it was. I was guilty of looking to the future and being pretty selfish about what I thought the future held for me.

These words from Oswald Chambers are a great reminder:

> *"We calculate and estimate, and say that this and that will happen, and we forget to make room for God to come in as He chooses…Do not look for God to come in any particular*

way but look for Him. That is the way to make room for Him. Expect Him to come, but do not expect Him in only a certain way. However much we may know of God, the great lesson to learn is that at any minute, He may break in. Always be in a state of expectancy and see that you leave room for God to come in as He likes."

Jesus asked blind Bartimaeus a very simple question: **"What do you want me to do for you?"** His need seems pretty obvious (see Luke 18:35-43). Others in the crowd could have probably answered the question, but Jesus wanted to hear His response.

TAKE UP: What do I want Jesus to do for me?

Bartimaeus answered Jesus' question in four words: "**I want to see.**"

Most of us carry around lists of things to do, and perhaps you have a long list of things you want Jesus to do for you. Today would be a great day to narrow your list to only one thing, then write it down, speak it out loud, and watch and see what God will do.

Reading for Reflection: Psalms 40:3; Jude 1:21

*I'm just waiting for God to tell me what to do,
but whatever it is, I want to be doing something like
I am doing now – serving God and helping people.*
Bethany Hamilton

◇◇◇

RISING DOUBTS

*Why are you troubled, and why do
doubts rise in your minds?*

Luke 24:38

There are two critical questions on a sign attached to the pylon of a bridge on the Welland River. The sign serves as a warning for boaters on this river that empties into the Niagara. While the water is fairly calm there, a short distance away are some treacherous rapids followed by the 180-foot drop at the American and Horseshoe Falls. The sign asks two questions:

Do you have an anchor? Do you know how to use it?

These are two great questions for someone boating near Niagara Falls and two great questions about the subject of doubt. Do you have an anchor? When the thunder booms and the lightning strikes in the storms of life, is there an anchor for your soul? Faith in God is an anchor, but what if I have doubts? What if I'm not sure? What if my personality is such that I question everything? The word doubt comes from the same root as the word "double." To doubt means to be double-minded, to have a divided mind in which a person wavers between believing and disbelieving. If we are honest, we would all admit that we have experienced or maybe are experiencing times of doubt.

Following His resurrection, Jesus asks His startled and disbelieving disciples (see Luke 24:36-49) a question about their emotional state and the depth of their faith. They were struggling to find an anchor and were perhaps still not quite sure how to use it. Another storm had come into their lives, filled with uncertainty about the future – their futures. Jesus acknowledges their fragile faith and the human tendency toward doubt but reminds them of the transformational power available because of the resurrection.

It is difficult to imagine what the disciples must have been feeling. Having just witnessed the news of Jesus' resurrection, their emotions must have run the gamut with a mixture of joy, fear, and disbelief. Their emotional turmoil reflects a common human experience – the struggle to reconcile faith with reality, particularly when faced with extraordinary events. It is often easier to cling to familiar narratives than to embrace the unexpected, even when that unexpected event is miraculous and life-changing.

Jesus offers a gentle invitation to overcome their fear and embrace the reality of what His resurrection meant for them and for everyone. He did not dismiss their emotions but addressed the root cause of their distress. Jesus recognized their confusion and invited them to move beyond their doubts and embrace the power of the resurrection. This conversation reminds us of the importance of confronting our doubts and fears. It is often more comfortable to remain in our uncertainty, but faith requires us to move beyond our doubts and embrace a deeper trust in God's promises.

TAKE UP: Am I allowing doubts to hinder my faith, or am I actively seeking to embrace the transformative power of Christ's resurrection? What steps might I take to fuel my faith and starve my fears?

Remember, doubt is not the opposite of faith; unbelief is. The disciples' fear and doubt are replaced with awe and understanding as they interact with the resurrected Jesus. We are transformed when we choose to engage fully with God's power and promises. Let's examine the doubts and fears in our hearts. May we be empowered to move beyond our uncertainty, embracing the truth of the resurrection and the hope it offers for our lives and our future. Let us strive to live with a faith that is unwavering, rooted in the knowledge that Jesus conquered death and offers us the gift of eternal life.

Reading for Reflection: 1 Kings 18:41-46; Jude 1:22

If faith never encounters doubt, if truth never struggles with error, if good never battles with evil, how can faith know its own power. If I have to choose between a faith that has stared doubt in the eye and made it blink, or a naïve faith that has never known the firing line of faith, I will choose the former every time.
Gary Parker

◇◇◇

FIXER UPPER

What is that to you?

John 21:22

Our culture has become fascinated by restoration. Don't believe me? Turn on the television and take your choice from among the following shows: *This Old House, Fixer Upper, Flip this House, Flea Market Flip, Renovation Raiders, American Restoration, American Pickers, Fast N' Loud, Counting Cars, Dream Cars, Rock My RV, Bar Rescue, Tank Overhaul, Divine Restoration,* and the list goes on. I confess that I love restoration, and it seems like most of my life I have been involved in restoration work.

Here's some truth: at some point in your life, you needed restoration, and I am convinced that the greatest need in our world today is for the restoration of the relationship with the Father that was designed at creation.

Webster's defines restoration as...

1. **To bring back into existence or use; reestablish**
2. **To bring back to an original condition**
3. **To put (someone) back in a former position**
4. **To make restitution of; give back**

At some point after the crucifixion and resurrection, Jesus cooks breakfast for Peter and some of the other disciples who were fishing (John 21:20-25). Jesus invites Peter for a walk, a restoration walk. Peter has denied Jesus, and we can only imagine what he might have been feeling as they strolled through the sand. Peter, as he was prone to do, interrupts Jesus and changes the subject, inquiring about the fate of John, the beloved disciple. Jesus responds and gently redirects shifting speculation about the momentary to a call for an unwavering commitment to following Him.

The future, in its unknown aspects, is ultimately in God's hands. We may have hopes, plans, and expectations, but God holds the ultimate authority over time and events. Trying to predict the future, particularly regarding others' lives, is futile and distracts us from our primary calling. Peter's concern for John, though born out of love and loyalty, maybe even some jealousy, reveals a potential focus on the temporal rather than the eternal. The emphasis shifts from wondering about John's earthly lifespan to the imperative of steadfast discipleship. Our focus should be on actively following Jesus, regardless of what the future may hold for ourselves or for others.

TAKE UP: Will my biggest concerns today be the same a month from now? A year? What steps can I take to lift my eyes from today to seeing the issues on a higher plane?

Surrender your need to control the future. Stop trying to map out your life, anticipating what might lie ahead. While planning and preparation are important, we cannot fully grasp or predict the future. Instead, we are called to trust in God's sovereignty and to follow His lead, day by day. Set aside your anxieties about the future and focus on our commitment to Christ. May we find peace in surrendering our need to control and find joy in the journey of following Jesus, wherever He may lead, trusting that His plan for our lives is perfect.

Reading for Reflection: Jeremiah 29:11-12; 2 Corinthians 4:16-18

You cannot escape the responsibility
of tomorrow by evading it today.
Abraham Lincoln

◇◇◇

BUILD UP

And it will be said: "Build up, build up, prepare the road!
Remove the obstacles out of the way of my people."
Isaiah 57:14

Extra Grace Required - Matthew 5:46

Marbles or Grapes - Matthew 6:25

Calling Home - Luke 2:49

Grumbling - John 6:61

Seize the Moment - Matthew 9:15

Flavor Enhancement - Mark 9:50

Sing! - Luke 12:25

Breakfast on the Beach - John 21:15

Campfires and Gnats - Matthew 23:17-19

◇◇◇

EXTRA GRACE REQUIRED

*If you love those who love you,
what reward will you get?*

Matthew 5:46

Some people are sooooooo much easier to love than others. Whether it is their personality, our personality, or some combination of the two, if we are honest, we find it easier to do life with some folks, and it is natural to choose to spend more time with them when given a choice. But life has a way of bringing some people into our lives that I've heard referred to as *extra grace required (EGR)* kind of people. Right now, pictures are going off in your mind as you read those words, and that's okay because we all have EGR people. What's really funny is that for others, we may be EGR people!

In Jesus' Sermon on the Mount, He redefines the standards of love and righteousness and His expectations about how we respond to those who cross our path and may live in our homes (see Matthew 43-48). At first glance, loving those who love us seems like a natural response. It's easy to reciprocate affection and kindness to those who treat us well. However, Jesus calls us to a higher standard – a radical love that extends beyond our comfort zones. By referencing tax collectors, who were notoriously viewed as sinners and outcasts, Jesus emphasizes that true love transcends societal norms and expectations.

This question invites us to reflect on our own hearts. Are we limiting our love only to those who are easy to love? Are there individuals or groups we find difficult to embrace? Jesus challenges us to break down these barriers, pushing us to love even those who may oppose us or treat us poorly. This kind of love is not dependent on the actions of others; it is grounded in the character of God and our commitment to reflect His love in the world.

BUILD UP: Who is the EGR person in my life and how could I love them in ways that would be a blessing for us both?

Loving beyond limits requires grace and humility and it invites us to see others through God's eyes, recognizing their inherent worth and the need for compassion. When we choose to love those who are different from us or even those who have wronged us, we embody the heart of Christ and become agents of transformation in our communities. Could we consider how we can cultivate a love that knows no boundaries? May we ask God to soften our hearts and enable us to love as He loves? In doing so, we fulfill the calling to be His disciples, shining light into the darkness and demonstrating His grace to a world in need.

Reading for Reflection: Proverbs 4:23; Ephesians 4:1-7

There is no exercise better for the heart than
reaching down and lifting people up.
John Andres Holmes

◇◇◇

MARBLES OR GRAPES?

Is not life more than food,
and the body more than clothes?

Matthew 6:25

Years ago, I loaned my car to my brother. This wasn't just any car; it was a beautiful midnight blue Chevrolet Corvette! I placed all kinds of restrictions on when and where he could drive this vehicle, which I so highly valued. Guess what he did? He wrecked it! Actually, it wasn't his fault, but an uninsured driver ran a red light and hit him. My brother was fine. The car was totaled. I was mad…more than just a little miffed, but God used those days to teach me about the power of possessions.

One of the great early lessons when the Christian church began was an understanding that they didn't really own anything. God owned it all. When they took a quick inventory of their lives, they decided that pooling their assets made sense and they created a sharing community. Would you have been comfortable in this community with no possessions of your own and sharing everything you have?

I think I would struggle in that kind of group. I want to be generous, and I understand that nothing I own is really mine, but sharing everything? It seems kind of radical to me, and my selfish spirit can quickly creep in. These days we don't have many communities that share all their possessions, and the truth is we don't have many communities that are one in heart and mind. But this passage teaches me a great truth:

People are more important than possessions, always.

I love what Anne Ortlund wrote about communities of faith: "You can choose to be a bag of marbles, single units that don't affect each other except in collision...or you can choose to be a bag of grapes. The juices begin to mingle, and there is no way to extricate yourselves if you tried. Each is part of all."

If you are in a community of faith, give thanks and celebrate this gift. If not, find one and be a grape!

BUILD UP: Am I good at sharing?

Sharing is one of the first lessons we are typically taught. For some people, it comes easier than others. It is a lesson I am still learning and one where I would like to excel. God loves extravagance and demonstrates it daily. Let's be contagious and hilarious givers sharing our blessings.

Reading for Reflection: Proverbs 21:26; Matthew 6:19-34

"Material possessions, winning scores,
and great reputations are meaningless in
the eyes of the Lord, because He knows what
we really are and that is all that matters."
Coach John Wooden

◇◇◇

CALLING HOME

*Didn't you know I had to be
in my Father's house?*

Luke 2:49

Walking through the university's Student Center, I was stopped by one of the newest students on campus who wanted to know what I was doing on a particular weekend in September. Uncertain about my calendar or his request I inquired to learn the reason for his question. His response was short and simple:

"I need you to be my Dad for that weekend."

My young friend was a member of the basketball team and each year in preparation for their season, the coaches led a father and son retreat, complete with the coaches' fathers in attendance, too. These adventures provided a time for the guys to eat unhealthy food, compete in a variety of games, take on some crazy undertakings, and make some lifelong memories. Without checking my calendar, I knew that I was in. Whatever the conflict, I would cancel. Whatever the obstacle, I would find a way to remove it. How can one say no to the opportunity to stand in for a young man whose father lives on another continent and who has no possibility of joining this annual expedition?

For years, I had heard powerful stories that came from these retreats but I had never experienced one. Now I have and the experience was even better than the stories. What a privilege to have a ringside seat to something very seldom seen or heard in our cyber-world of text messaging, social media, and the Velcro-like attachment of our "smart" phones.

As a guy who grew up without a father, the weekend created all sorts of emotions for me and reminded me of how grateful I am that God sent some wonderful men along as "borrowed Dads" along the way.

Over the course of a few hours that weekend, I witnessed earthly fathers doing their best imitation of their Heavenly Father. Their prayers, their words of affirmation, and their hugs and high-fives gave me hope and encouraged me to wish that for every boy and girl, regardless of their age.

If you study the life of Jesus' time on earth, you will discover that He was a son who liked to call home. On a regular basis, we find Jesus calling home to talk to His Father. When his disciples asked him for help in learning how to pray, He offered the model prayer that most of us know as the Lord's Prayer. Jesus didn't teach His disciples this prayer to be used as some kind of packaged devotional or a "Get Out of Jail Free Card." He wants it to be a model for regular calls to our heavenly home.

BUILD UP: Have I developed an ongoing running conversation with God?

I confess to you that I understand prayer about as well as I understand how a "smart" phone works, or any phone for that matter. But my lack of understanding does not prevent me from using a telephone, nor does it prevent me from praying. I love it when my kids call home. It makes my day. And now my granddaughters call, always a blessing! Whether they need something or just want to talk, I'm always eager to hear from them, and I believe beyond a shadow of a doubt that the same is true for our heavenly Father. Call home!

Reading for Reflection: 2 Chronicles 7:14; Luke 11:1-4

For prayer is nothing else than
being on terms of friendship with God.
St. Teresa of Avila

◇◇◇

GRUMBLING

Does this offend you?

John 6:61

We've all said things that offended someone else, sometimes on purpose while others were completely unintentional. Count me among those who have on more than one occasion opened my mouth and inserted my foot. Apologizing for words of offense is never fun, but oh so important and not the easiest thing to do. Jesus spoke words that sometimes offended, but never to hurt, always to help.

I love the transparency of this question as His radical message had challenged the understanding of His followers and caused grumbling (see John 6:60-66). He was well aware of the words and emotions created among those who at this point saw Him only as a great teacher. Why would He say some of the things He was saying, like *"eating My flesh"* and *"drinking My blood?"* Weird, don't you think, especially for this first-century audience.

Jesus often confronted the norms and expectations of His audience. His teachings pushed them beyond their comfort zones, inviting them to grapple with deeper spiritual truths. When faced with difficulty or offense, many disciples struggled to accept what He was saying. This encounter serves as a reminder that following Christ is not always easy or straightforward. There will be moments when His teachings challenge our beliefs, confront our lifestyles, or call us to deeper faith.

In our own lives, we may find ourselves wrestling with aspects of our faith that are difficult to accept. Perhaps it is the call to forgive those who have wronged us, to love our enemies, or to trust God in times of uncertainty. These teachings can provoke discomfort and require us to step out of our comfort zones. However, it is in these moments of discomfort that we often experience the most significant growth.

BUILD UP: Am I struggling with a Scripture that defies cultural norms or a personal interpretation? Am I willing to dig deeper and study this truth, or have I cast it aside and tried to pretend it is not in God's Word?

Jesus invites us to confront our doubts and questions, encouraging us to engage with His truth even when it is hard. He invites us to bring our struggles to Him, knowing that He understands our human frailty. When we do this, we open the door to deeper understanding and a stronger faith. Let us embrace the hard teachings of Christ with open hearts. May we seek to understand rather than retreat in discomfort, trusting that through our struggles, God is shaping us into His image. In our willingness to engage with the difficult aspects of faith, we find the path to true discipleship and transformation.

Reading for Reflection: Psalms 115:1-11; 2 Timothy 2:22-26

The question to be asked of all teaching is not,
'Is it new?' but 'Is it true?'
F.F. Bruce

◇◇◇

SEIZE THE MOMENT

*How can the guests of the bridegroom
mourn while he is with them?*

Matthew 9:15

President Theodore Roosevelt is credited with saying, *"comparison is the thief of joy,"* though there is no evidence that he ever offered those words. Regardless, I love the quote and believe it is so true. Comparison creeps into most of our lives, whether it relates to what we see from our next-door neighbors, the giftings of a talented co-worker, or a beautiful new automobile stopped at the red light next to us. We look, we wonder, we compare, and sometimes we covet; and often we complain.

John the Baptizer had his own set of disciples and one day they got to comparing their fasting practices with those of Jesus' disciples, and that leads to asking Jesus why His disciples were such slackers (my words, not theirs). Jesus responds with a seemingly simple statement inviting them to discover new truths about the nature of joy, sorrow, and the appropriate response to different seasons of life.

Jesus uses the powerful metaphor of a wedding feast to illustrate the appropriate response to His presence (see Matthew 9:14-17). A wedding celebration is a time of joy, feasting, and rejoicing. Fasting, a practice of abstaining from food for spiritual reasons, is typically associated with mourning or repentance. Jesus points out the incongruity of fasting while He is present, emphasizing that His presence should be a time of celebration and joy. Jesus was a faster, He not only practiced it, but He also recommended it. As He speaks to John's disciples, He is not condemning fasting but highlighting the importance of recognizing and responding appropriately to the moment.

There is a time for rejoicing and a time for mourning. Jesus' ministry was a time of great joy, healing, and the proclamation of God's kingdom. It was a time to celebrate the arrival of the Messiah and to embrace the hope He brought. Jesus knew that a time of sorrow and mourning was coming. His death and crucifixion were inevitable, and there would be a time for His followers to fast, to reflect, and to mourn the loss of their friend and teacher. The metaphor underscores the importance of discerning the appropriate response in each season of life.

BUILD UP: What moments and opportunities am I missing because I'm too busy comparing, maybe even complaining?

The presence of Christ should be a time of celebration of gratitude for His sacrifice and His love. Yet, there will be times of difficulty, loss, and suffering, and in those moments, it is a time to reflect, pray, and seek God's comfort. Consider this: are we living in a spirit of gratitude and celebration for the presence of Christ in our lives? And when sorrow comes, are we turning to Him for comfort and guidance? May we be sensitive to the different seasons of life, responding with joy, faith, and trust in God's plan.

Reading for Reflection: Haggai 2:1-5; 2 Corinthians 3:10

Write it on your heart that every day is the best day in the year.
Ralph Waldo Emerson

◇◇◇

FLAVOR ENHANCEMENT

Salt is good, but if it loses its saltiness,
how can you make it salty again?

Mark 9:50

A great friend of mine reaches for the salt every time the food arrives in a restaurant. Even though he has not tasted the meal yet, he is certain that salt needs to be added. Even after half a century of friendship and hundreds of times of questioning him about this behavior, he continues to grab the salt. Fortunately, he doesn't suffer from any high blood pressure and his love of salt has not had any adverse effects on his health. He simply loves salt, the more, the better.

Salt has a super interesting history in our world. Long before refrigeration, salt was vital for preserving meat, fish, and other perishable goods. This made it invaluable for trade and survival, particularly for populations distant from readily available sources. Access to salt often defined the prosperity of communities and empires. The Romans paid their armies partly in salt ("salarium," the root for the word "salary"). In addition to being a preservative and payment, it was and is a flavor enhancer making things taste better, especially tortilla chips!

Jesus used salt as a powerful metaphor for the transformative influence of faith in a person's life. Just as salt preserves and seasons, faith purifies and enriches our character, preserving us from spiritual decay and enhancing our interactions with others. But in this exchange with His disciples (see Mark 9:42-50), Jesus points out that salt can lose its saltiness. This implies a loss of spiritual vitality and a decline in the transformative power of faith. When we allow the distractions of the world to cloud our hearts, when we neglect our relationship with God, or when we fail to live out the teachings of Jesus, we can lose the saltiness that makes us effective witnesses for Him. This loss of saltiness is not a sudden event but a gradual process that can lead to spiritual apathy and disengagement.

BUILD UP: Do I possess the saltiness of faith, allowing it to preserve me spiritually and enhance my interactions with others? Am I nurturing my relationship with God and promoting peace within my community?

When we prioritize our relationship with Him, we become vessels of His grace, enabling us to make a positive impact on the world around us. Let's nurture our relationship with God through prayer, study of Scripture, and fellowship with other believers. Just as salt enhances flavor, harmony and peace within our communities enhances our effectiveness in witnessing to the world. Disagreements and conflicts can hinder our ability to share the Gospel and reflect Christ's love. May we strive to live in a way that reflects the transformative power of Christ, allowing our faith to be a source of preservation and harmony in our lives and in the lives of those around us.

Reading for Reflection: 2 Kings 2:19-22; Colossians 4:6

Sometimes we need the salt of tears to remind
us how to savor the sweetness of life.
Lysa TerKeurst

◇◇◇

SING!

*Who of you by worrying can
add a single hour to your life?*

Luke 12:25

The song "Don't Worry, Be Happy" became a hit back in 1988. Written and performed by Bobby McFerrin, the song had everyone singing out loud! The lyrics were simple, the melody was catchy and upbeat, and the message encouraged everyone to maintain a positive attitude in the face of life's challenges. Though not a musician, I loved the song and felt my spirit rise each time it came on the radio. But let's be honest: not worrying is hard, harder for some than for others. It may be the circumstances faced, the personality you were gifted, or simply a choice to travel the road of worry. Whatever the reason, worry is a path most of us walk at some season in our lives.

Jesus asks a question that invites us to examine the nature of worry and its impact on our lives(see Luke 12:22-31). He recognized that worrying is a common human experience, yet He also points out its futility. Worry often consumes our thoughts and can lead us to a place of anxiety and fear. We may find ourselves preoccupied with what tomorrow holds – whether it be financial concerns, health issues, or relationship struggles. However, Jesus reminds us that worrying accomplishes nothing. In fact, it often detracts from our ability to live fully in the present moment, where God's grace and provision await us.

We have an invitation, perhaps a challenge, to shift our focus from our worries to our faith. Instead of allowing anxiety to dominate our thoughts, we are invited to trust in God's sovereignty and care. Jesus encourages us to look at the birds of the air and the lilies of the field, which God provides for abundantly without effort or worry. If God takes care of these creations, how much more will He care for us, His beloved children? Worry weakens us, and it is often contagious, spreading like a virus to our family and friends.

BUILD UP: What am I worried about today, and what is the obstacle that is keeping me from giving it to God and not picking it back up?

Years ago, I heard someone say that the only antidote to worry is prayer. Let us consider how we can let go of our worries and embrace a posture of trust by kneeling in prayer. Surrender your concerns, by voice, by writing them down and then tearing them up, and by placing your faith in Him. Truly, we can experience peace that transcends understanding, freeing us from the burdens of anxiety.

While we cannot control our circumstances, we can control our response. Instead of worrying, we can choose to pray, seeking God's guidance and peace. In doing so, we align ourselves with His will and open our hearts to His provision. As we meditate on this passage, let us cast our cares upon Him, knowing that He is faithful and always present in our lives.

Reading for Reflection: 2 Kings 19:1-16; 1 Peter 5:6-7

Worry does not empty tomorrow of its sorrow.
It empties today of its strength.
Corrie Ten Boom

◇◇◇

BREAKFAST ON THE BEACH

...do you love me more than these?

John 21:15

Breakfast cooked outdoors and a walk on a beach with a friend – does it get any better? Count me among those who believe breakfast is not only the most important meal of the day, but it is the best one. And while I've never quite answered the question about what I prefer most, beach or mountains, I love to walk, and beaches are exceptional places for a stroll because they are constantly changing. The tide comes in, goes out, and brings with it an assortment of treasures to examine.

The context for this question is Jesus as a short-order cook and now hiking companion for Simon Peter (see John 21:1-19). Jesus gets the conversation started with a question about "these," and we don't know exactly what he was referring to. One common understanding is that "these" refers to the other disciples. Jesus is asking Peter if his love for Him surpasses the bonds and relationships he shares with his fellow followers. This emphasizes the primacy of love for Christ above all other earthly relationships and commitments.

Another interpretation suggests that "these" refers to the physical possessions or the fishing business Peter and the others had returned to after Jesus' resurrection. In this view, Jesus is challenging Peter to consider whether his love for Christ and his calling is greater than his attachment to his previous way of life, which signifies a call to prioritize spiritual pursuits over material ones.

Both interpretations highlight the theme of commitment and the nature of true discipleship. Jesus is not only seeking affirmation of Peter's love but also challenging him to evaluate his priorities. This question serves as a pivotal moment for Peter, as it calls him to reflect on his loyalty and the depth of his devotion. Ultimately, Jesus' question is a profound invitation to all believers to examine their own hearts. It reminds us that our love for Christ should be the foundation upon which all other relationships and pursuits are built. When we place Jesus at the center of our lives, we find purpose and direction in our service to Him and others.

BUILD UP: What about my stuff, my family, my friends - is my priority Jesus, or have I set my affections on something or someone that moves Him to second or third place?

As followers of Christ, we are called to *"feed My (His) sheep."* We can do this in so many ways: providing encouragement to a friend, serving in our communities, or sharing the Gospel with those who have yet to know Him. Our love for Jesus should compel us to look beyond ourselves and serve others, reflecting His compassion and grace. Let us remember that love in action is the hallmark of our faith, and through our service, we bring glory to God.

Reading for Reflection: Joshua 23:6-11; Mark 12:30

Though our feelings come and go, God's love for us does not.
C.S. Lewis

◇◇◇

CAMPFIRE AND GNATS

*Which is greater: the gold,
or the temple that makes the gold sacred?
Which is greater: the gift, or the altar
that makes the gift sacred?*

Matthew 23:17-19

Count me among those who hopes camps for children and youth will remain a valid and viable tradition in the years to come. As an eight-year-old I knelt at an altar somewhere in central Florida during a children's camp. My mother loved to tell the story that she packed my suitcase with individual outfits in clear plastic bags so that it would be easy for me to change clothes each day. Her version of the story is that I returned home in the same clothes I wore to camp with all the plastic bags unopened. I dispute that story, though the two memories I have of that camp were trusting Jesus as my Savior and gnats. A relationship with Jesus was great, the gnats, not so much. This campground was infested with gnats, and the only time we got any relief was around the campfire at night. Apparently, the gnats did not like campfires. I like campfires, and I love camps where people find Jesus.

Jesus talked about gnats and camels while confronting hypocrisy with a series of what my Bible calls the *Seven Woes on the Teachers of the Law and Pharisees* (see Matthew 23:13-39). The questions He asked exposed the corruption that can arise when human traditions supersede divine commands. The imagery of straining out a gnat and swallowing a camel is particularly striking. It illustrates the absurdity of focusing on minor details of the Law while neglecting its core principles. The Pharisees were meticulous about following the minutiae of religious tradition, yet they disregarded the more significant aspects of justice, mercy, and compassion. Their actions highlight the danger of legalism – an overemphasis on rules and regulations that overshadows the heart of faith.

Jesus didn't mince words, *"You shut the kingdom of heaven in men's faces. You yourselves do not enter, nor will you let those enter who are trying to."* Their self-righteousness prevented them from embracing the truth of Jesus' message and blocked others from experiencing God's grace. They held onto their traditions so tightly that they became obstacles to genuine faith. Following Jesus was never intended to be easy, but the invitation to a relationship was not designed to be an obstacle path. We want to open the way for all men and women to enter the kingdom of heaven.

BUILD UP: What traditions or practices am I clinging to that hinder my spiritual growth? Have I created barriers to faith for myself and others? How can I share the gospel in ways that attract others to come to know Jesus personally?

May we strive to live in a way that reflects the heart of Christ, prioritizing genuine faith over outward conformity. Let us be willing to examine our beliefs, ensuring they align with God's will, and be open to the transformative power of His love. Let's invest in camps, even those with gnats, but let's not act like a gnat trying to swallow a camel.

Reading for Reflection: Ruth 4:1-12; Galatians 2:20

How wonderful to know that Christianity is more than a padded pew or a dim cathedral, but that it is a real, living, daily experience which goes on from grace to grace.
Jim Elliot

◇◇◇

TREASURE UP

*But Mary treasured up all these things
and pondered them in her heart.*

Luke 2:19

The Best of Times - Luke 12:56-57

Church Picnics - John 6:5

Pick Me - John 6:70

Fiddling - Matthew 15:3

Good Trades - Matthew 16:26

Dog With a Bone - Luke 18:7

Street Sweeper - Luke 22:27

Enduring Love - John 21:17

Small Stuff - Luke 16:11

Power Surge - Matthew 26:53

◇◇◇

THE BEST OF TIMES

How is it that you don't know how to interpret this present time? Why don't you judge for yourselves what is right?

Luke 12:56-57

Awareness, especially self-awareness, is such an important asset in following God's plan for our lives. A Wednesday lunch Bible study with some seasoned citizens taught me this truth in a powerful way. Alice, dressed in a bright pink sweater even in the midst of Houston's heat and humidity, was a regular participant in this weekly gathering. On this particular day, I asked these saints to share about the best time of their lives. As they took turns we heard stories of births and marriages and graduations and exotic vacations, but then we came to Alice, who was last but not least, and certainly the most memorable. She answered with two words: *"Right now."* Surprising, yes, but not really. Though she was in her early 90s, suffering from arthritis, and living a quiet life with her daughter, I knew Alice to be one of the most discerning people I had ever met. She was content, she was present, and she was most grateful for all that God had given her in life.

Jesus poses some seemingly simple questions near the end of Luke 12 (see Luke 12:54-59) that reveal deep truths about spiritual discernment, personal responsibility, and the importance of actively engaging with faith. He knew that the ability to discern right from wrong is a crucial aspect of faith, requiring careful study of Scripture, prayerful reflection, and the guidance of the Holy Spirit. It is not about imposing our own standards but about aligning our lives with God's will. The question urges us to move beyond blindly following traditions or cultural norms and actively engaging with God's Word. We must develop our spiritual discernment, allowing the Holy Spirit to guide us in making wise decisions. This involves studying scripture, prayer, and seeking counsel from trusted spiritual leaders. It is not a call to self-reliance but a call to actively engage in the process of seeking God's guidance.

Jesus also reminded the crowd of the importance of preparation and thoughtful engagement with our faith. He challenged the notion of passive faith, where we simply accept what we hear without critical reflection. Instead, faith calls for active engagement, careful consideration, and a willingness to discuss and explore our beliefs with others.

TREASURE UP: Am I actively engaging with God's Word, seeking His guidance, and discussing my beliefs thoughtfully with others? Am I listening for His voice to direct and guide me in ways that illuminate my path and bless others?

This call to discussion is not about promoting division or argument but rather fostering a deeper understanding of our faith and strengthening our commitment to it. Engaging in meaningful conversations with others allows us to grow in our knowledge, to refine our understanding, and to sharpen our ability to articulate our faith to those around us. May we strive to cultivate personal discernment, allowing the Holy Spirit to guide our lives. May we be prepared to share our faith with clarity and conviction, reflecting the truth and love of Christ to a world in need.

Reading for Reflection: Judges 21:25; Hebrews 5:11-14

Discernment is God's call to intercession, never to faultfinding.
Corrie Ten Boom

◇◇◇

CHURCH PICNICS

*Where shall we buy bread
for these people to eat?*

John 6:5

An invitation to a church picnic during my teenage years led to thousands of relationships and ultimately God's call on my life into Christian ministry. Never in my wildest dreams could I have imagined all the opportunities God would give, and in so many ways, it started in a county park with a bunch of strangers. While I do not remember much about that day, other than catching a snake in a creek, I am confident that loaves of bread and fish were not on the menu. Well, maybe a few loaves to cover the hot dogs, but no fish.

Of all the stories in the Bible, the miracle of the little boy with the picnic lunch ranks at or near the top of my list (see John 6:1-15). Though I can't prove it, I'm convinced there was more food in the crowd that day, but only one young guy was willing to share. He was certain that Jesus could do more with his lunch than anyone else could imagine, so he willingly released it.

An enormous crowd approached Jesus and He chose, I believe, to make this a teaching moment for one of His disciples. He turned to Philip with a seemingly simple yet significant question about feeding them. This was not merely a logistical inquiry; it was an invitation for Philip – and us – to reflect on faith, provision, and the nature of God's abundance. Philip faced an overwhelming situation. Over five thousand people were hungry, and the resources at hand were minimal. Jesus' question to him highlights a critical aspect of faith: recognizing our limitations while trusting in God's ability to provide. Philip's response was pragmatic but limited, revealing his focus on scarcity rather than abundance.

Like Philip, we often see what we don't have instead of doing an asset inventory and celebrating what God has provided. Let's be honest, we often find ourselves in circumstances that seem insurmountable. Whether it's financial strain, health challenges, or relational conflicts, acknowledging our limitations is the first step toward experiencing God's provision. Here's an idea: Shift your perspective and instead of focusing solely on what you lack, consider what God has given you. Just as Jesus took the small offering of loaves and fish and multiplied it, He can take our little and make it much.

TREASURE UP: What resources, talents, or connections has God already gifted me? Am I using what I've been given? Will I trust Him when I need more?

Here's the part of the story I love the most. Jesus didn't ask Philip to solve the problem alone. Instead, He wanted Philip to lean into the possibility of divine intervention. When faced with challenges, remind yourself that God's resources are limitless. Pray and ask God to help you see beyond your circumstances and trust His provision. We serve a God of abundance and One who has invited us to pray about anything and everything. As we recognize our limitations, may we also see the possibilities God has placed before us. May we learn to trust in His goodness and rely on His provision for every aspect of our life. We know, because of a young boy, that God can multiply even the smallest of offerings.

Reading for Reflection: Psalms 77:11; Matthew 13:58

There are only two ways to live your life. One is as though nothing is a miracle. The other is as though everything is a miracle.
Albert Einstein

◇◇◇

PICK ME

Have I not chosen you?

John 6:70

Can you remember the joy or maybe the pain when sides were chosen for a game on an elementary playground or athletic field? How about later in life when you competed for a job and the search committee selected someone else? I've experienced a wide range of emotions when it comes to the process of being chosen, or being notified that though I was a finalist, I was not the first choice of the committee. And over the years I've consoled and counseled a number of friends who competed for a position only to suffer the agony of defeat. Here is what I've discovered: Everyone wants to be chosen! Even if it is a team that you really don't want to join or an assignment that doesn't seem to be the right fit, we love to be chosen. It is in our DNA, and when someone else is selected, it hurts.

Jesus reminds His disciples that they were hand-picked, invited to follow Him, and selected by the one who would become their Savior (see John 6:60-71). His question comes during some discouraging moments for His disciples. Many of His followers had turned away, disheartened by His teachings. Jesus, fully aware of the impending betrayal by Judas Iscariot, highlights the complexity of human relationships and the reality of betrayal even among those closest to Him.

This question Jesus poses challenges us to reflect on the nature of our own relationships and the potential for disappointment. Jesus chose His disciples, investing in them deeply, yet one of them would ultimately betray Him. It serves as a sobering reminder that even in our most trusted circles, there can be moments of disloyalty or misunder-standing. The presence of betrayal can leave us feeling vulnerable and heartbroken.

But this passage also reveals the incredible grace and love of Jesus. Despite knowing Judas' intentions, He continued to teach, to reach out, and to demonstrate love. This challenges us to respond to betrayal not with bitterness, but with the grace Jesus exemplified. In our lives, we may encounter betrayal from friends, family, or colleagues. When this happens, we have a choice: to dwell in hurt or to extend forgiveness and understanding. Jesus' acknowledgment of Judas reminds us that we are all capable of making choices that can lead us astray. We must remain vigilant in our own hearts, seeking to align ourselves with God's will rather than succumbing to temptation.

TREASURE UP: Have I been betrayed and failed to move forward or am I stuck in the past reliving the story, afraid to trust again? Have I quit taking risks because I am afraid I might not be chosen? Let us embrace the lessons of grace, vigilance, and love in examining how Jesus served His disciples. May we strive to be faithful in our relationships, extending the same grace we receive from Christ. In moments of betrayal, let us remember Jesus' example and choose to respond with love, trusting in God's greater plan.

Reading for Reflection: Isaiah 53; Acts 10:37-38

David was the last one we would have chosen to
fight the giant, but he was chosen of God.
Dwight L. Moody

◇◇◇

FIDDLING

Why do you break the command of
God for the sake of your tradition?

Matthew 15:3

The song *"Tradition"* is the opening number of the musical *"Fiddler on the Roof,"* and it captured my attention the very first time I heard it as a sophomore in high school. One of the main characters, Tevye, a Jewish milkman living in the early 20th century in the fictional village of Anatevka, introduces the central theme of the musical: the importance of tradition within his community. The song outlines the roles and expectations of the various members of the family and the community, emphasizing how tradition shapes their lives and relationships. Tevye explains how tradition provides stability, identity, and continuity in a rapidly changing world. As a history major, count me among those who love tradition.

Jesus confronts the Pharisees and teachers of the law with a challenging question about tradition, a value they placed as their highest priority (see Matthew 15:1-9). The question Jesus asks highlights the tension between human traditions and divine commandments, emphasizing the importance of prioritizing God's truth over established practices. The Pharisees were focused on ceremonial cleanliness and the traditions that had developed over time. They had created a set of rules that often overshadowed the core principles of love, mercy, and obedience to God. Jesus' question serves as a wake-up call, urging them – and us – to examine the motivations behind our actions and the traditions we uphold.

Traditions can be valuable, providing structure and continuity within our faith communities. However, when they become more important than the commandments of God, they can lead us astray. Jesus calls us to evaluate the practices we follow.

TREASURE UP: Are my traditions rooted in Scripture and God's will, or have they become mere rituals that distract me from a genuine relationship with Him? Is there a tradition I need to re-examine or cast aside?

Back to the song *"Tradition"* for a moment. In the musical it foreshadows the conflicts and challenges that arise as younger generations begin to question and challenge the traditions of their parents and grandparents. This tension between tradition and change is a recurring theme throughout the musical, ultimately reflecting the struggles of many immigrant communities trying to balance their cultural identity with the pressures of a modern society. I see the challenge of tradition in the church today, and I remind us that Jesus challenges us to let go of anything that hinders our walk with Him.

In a world filled with distractions and competing priorities, let us commit to seeking God's truth above all else. May we strive to embody His love and grace, allowing His Word to shape our actions and beliefs. As we prioritize our relationship with God, we can engage in practices that draw us closer to Him and reflect His heart to the world around us.

Reading for Reflection: Deuteronomy 6:1-9; Colossians 2:8

Traditions tell us where we have come from. Scripture itself is
a better guide as to where we should now be going.
N.T. Wright

◇◇◇

GOOD TRADES

*What good will it be for someone to
gain the whole world, yet forfeit
his soul? Or what can anyone give
in exchange for their soul?*

Matthew 16:26

My children, my grandchildren, and the university students I get to hang out with receive some regular unsolicited advice from me. It is simple, not that profound, but in my opinion, incredibly important. Are you ready? Here it is: MAKE GOOD TRADES! I remind these people I love that life is all about trades, so we should make good ones. Some students trade sleep for grades, and others trade grades for sleep, and report cards reveal the rewards or the results. If we have two job options, one with higher pay and a long commute and the other keeping us close to home but providing less income, our choice between the jobs is a trade. My advice: **Make Good Trades**.

Of all the questions Jesus asks, Matthew 16:26 may be the most critical. Lovingly confronting His disciples, Jesus' question challenges the common human tendency to prioritize material gain and worldly success above all else. Culture creates a narrative leading us to pursue wealth, power, and recognition, believing that these things will bring us happiness and fulfillment. We invest our time, energy, and resources in accumulating possessions, pursuing careers, and building reputations. Yet, Jesus challenges us to consider the ultimate cost (trade) of such pursuits.

The *"whole world"* represents everything a person might desire in this life – wealth, fame, power, comfort. Yet, Jesus reminds His disciples, then and now, that *"forfeiting one's soul"* – is a loss far greater than any worldly gain, a very bad trade. Pursuing worldly things, at the expense of our spiritual well-being, is a tragic exchange. It is a life lived without purpose, without connection to God, and without the hope of eternal life.

Jesus' question requires us to evaluate our priorities. Are we investing our lives in things that will ultimately fade away, or are we building on a solid foundation of faith? The things of this world are temporary; they offer fleeting pleasures and momentary satisfaction. But our relationship with God, our commitment to His will, and our pursuit of righteousness are eternal. They offer lasting joy, peace, and the hope of eternal life.

TREASURE UP: As I examine my life, am I making good trades? Are there places and spaces that need change?

The price of neglecting our spiritual lives is too high. There is nothing in this world valuable enough to trade for our eternal destiny. This is not a message of fear or condemnation but a call to wakefulness. Let's examine the direction of our lives, realign our priorities, if necessary, and pursue a life of faith that honors God and brings lasting fulfillment. May we choose to invest in what is eternal, recognizing that our relationship with Christ is the most precious possession we have.

Reading for Reflection: Psalms 27:4; 1 John 5:11-13

I can't help but tell people of the greatest story ever told –
God's love and our eternal life.
David Green

◇◇◇

DOG WITH A BONE

*And will not God bring about justice for His
chosen ones, who cry out to Him day
and night? Will He keep putting them off?*

Luke 18:7

My grandfather had a thousand memorable expressions (or so it seemed to me), and one of my favorites was: *"He wouldn't give up. He was like a dog with a bone!"* As a child, I'm not sure I understood the concept, but I came to realize it was all about persistence. If we hang on and don't give up, even when others may be telling us to throw in the towel, good things often happen.

Jesus' question in Luke 18 comes from one of his parables, in this case, the story of a widow who persevered in prayer and a deep belief in the unwavering nature of God's justice (see Luke 18:1-8). The widow represents those who may feel powerless or overlooked in the face of adversity. She persistently seeks justice from an unjust judge, not because he is kind or fair, but because she refuses to give up. Her tenacity serves as a model for us, reminding us that perseverance in prayer is crucial. Jesus reassures us that, unlike the judge, God is a loving Father who cares deeply for His children. He hears our cries and responds to our needs.

This passage challenges us to consider how we approach God in prayer. When faced with struggles, do we turn to Him with persistence, or do we grow weary and lose faith? Jesus encourages us to cry out to God day and night, to bring our concerns before Him consistently. He wants us to know that our prayers matter and that our faithfulness in seeking Him will not go unnoticed.

God is just and faithful. When we feel like our prayers are falling on deaf ears, we can trust that God is working behind the scenes, always working on both ends of the situation, orchestrating events for our good. His timing may not align with ours, but His promises are sure.

TREASURE UP: What prayer have I been committed to praying and will continue to pray because it is that important?

Let us embrace the call to persistent prayer. Let us remember that God is attentive to our needs, and in due time, He will bring about justice and resolution. Trusting in His faithfulness allows us to approach Him boldly, knowing He is always ready to listen.

Reading for Reflection: 1 Samuel 1:1-18; 1 Thessalonians 5:16-18

The value of persistent prayer is not that He will
hear us but that we will finally hear Him.
William McGill

◇◇◇

STREET SWEEPER

For who is greater, the one who
is at the table or the one who serves?

Luke 22:27

The Magic Kingdom – Disney World. It was about 9:10 pm and our sur-viving party of three (the other three had headed back to the resort after a long day in the park) had staked out a spot to view the fireworks that begin each night at 9:20 pm. We were hundreds of yards from the castle with a good but slightly obstructed view, our position being determined by our decision to ride as many rides as possible before the show began instead of setting up camp an hour or two earlier to secure one of the prime viewing locations. We had taken our positions, await-ing the start of the show, when I felt a tap on my shoulder. I turned to find a uniformed Disney World employee standing in front of me. She had a simple question: "Would you like a better spot to view the fire-works?" Of course, my answer was yes, but I couldn't imagine how my new friend, Sarah, could help. You see, Sarah had a broom in one hand and a standing dustpan in the other. Did Sarah know some special spot that most park visitors overlook? Was Sarah having fun at our expense because we had waited so long to find a viewing location? Could Sarah be in an episode of *Undercover Boss* or was she really the Mayor of the Magic Kingdom?

We discovered that Sarah was a seventeen-year employee of Dis-ney World who really swept up trash across the park, but someone had given her the power to practice unreasonable hospitality, and she was about to bless us by giving us more than we could have ever expected.

We dutifully followed Sarah towards the castle. We passed through a couple of areas blocked off to the public. Other employees never questioned what Sarah was doing or why she was leading the three of us through their secured spaces. We arrived at our destination, a roped-off area within 50 yards of the castle, and two minutes later, the fireworks spectacular began. We looked at each other in disbelief wondering silently and out loud what we did to deserve such good fortune. When the show was over, we hugged Sarah, thanked her profusely, and even took pictures with her. We had been given more than we expected!

Jesus is preparing to face the cross, yet He takes the time to teach His disciples about true greatness through servanthood (see Luke 22:24-30). He gives them more than they could have ever expected. His disciples had been arguing about who among them was the greatest - for them it was about status and recognition. Jesus, however, flips the script. He emphasizes that greatness in His Kingdom is not about position or power but about humility and service to others.

Jesus healed the sick, welcomed the outcasts, and ultimately washed the disciples' feet – all acts of service that demonstrated His love and compassion. By identifying Himself as a servant, Jesus showed us that leadership in God's eyes is rooted in selflessness and the desire to lift others up.

TREASURE UP: What am I known for? Do others see me as a giver or a taker? How can I make service a daily devotion and not an occasional duty?

In a world that often glorifies ambition and power, Jesus calls us to embrace a different path – a path of humility and service. Remember, when we serve others, we embody the character of Christ. Our willingness to put others first can bring hope and healing to those around us, reflecting the heart of God in a tangible way. Let's ask God to cultivate a servant's heart within us. May we be inspired to look for opportunities to serve, to love, and to give of ourselves without seeking a reward.

Reading for Reflection: Psalms 33:16-22; Mark 10:45

*If a man is called to be a street sweeper,
he should sweep streets even as Michelangelo painted,
or Beethoven composed music, or Shakespeare wrote poetry.
He should sweep streets so well that all the hosts
of heaven and earth will pause to say, here lived
a great street sweeper who did his job well.*
Martin Luther King

◇◇◇

ENDURING LOVE

Do you love me?

John 21:17

We call our youngest granddaughter, Baylin, the "sweet bumble-bee," a nickname that she has thoroughly embraced. In fact, she has asked, sometimes demanded, that her classmates, teammates, and teachers use this name when calling her, all the more amazing when you know that she is only five years of age! While there are so many things I love about this little girl, my favorite is how out of the clear blue, she will say, *"Pop, you know what?" "No, Baylin, what?" "I love you."* Unsolicited, but never underappreciated, Baylin has no hesitation in expressing her love with words and affection.

Can you imagine asking someone if they loved you? Seems awkward, doesn't it? Yet that is exactly the question Jesus asks of Simon Peter while walking on the beach (see John 21:15-19). The disciple with a propensity for placing his foot in his mouth has denied Jesus three times, as predicted, and now the two of them are walking and talking. The opportunity is there for restoration, and Jesus' love for the extroverted disciple is on full display. It is a pivotal moment in Peter's post-resurrection experience. When asked, Peter affirms his love for Jesus, and then Jesus gives him instructions: *"Feed my sheep."* This seemingly simple command reveals a deeper truth about discipleship, leadership, and the responsibility of caring for others. Jesus entrusts Peter with the responsibility of caring for His followers, highlighting the importance of his leadership and service as Christian community is about to be birthed. It was more than preaching or teaching; it involved nurturing, guiding, and supporting others in their faith journey. It's a call to pastoral care, to actively tend to the needs of the flock.

Every single one of us has a role in the body of Christ. Jesus' words to Peter are a call to each of us to consider our responsibility to care for one another. This involves being present for others in times of need, offering guidance and support, praying and bearing each others' needs, and fostering a community of love and acceptance. Remember, actions speak louder than words.

TREASURE UP: Would I have a passionate and enthusiastic answer to the question Jesus asked Simon Peter? Have I accepted the call of Jesus to feed His sheep? What am I doing to nurture and support others in their faith?

It's not enough to simply say we love Jesus. Our love must be demonstrated through our commitment to love and our willingness to live out the teachings of Jesus. True love is active, compassionate, and selfless. May we be challenged to examine our own commitment to Christ and our responsibility to serve others. May we be inspired to nurture and support those around us, reflecting the love and compassion of our Shepherd. Let us actively seek opportunities to serve, to encourage, and to build up the body of Christ.

Reading for Reflection: Isaiah 58:8; 2 Corinthians 13:9-11

Broken things can be made whole again,
often stronger and more beautiful than before.
Unknown

◇◇◇

SMALL STUFF

*So if you have not been trustworthy
in handling worldly wealth, who will
trust you with true riches?*

Luke 16:11

A friend of mine has a favorite expression, one he has used so often that his family had a tee shirt made with the message:

Use it Up – Wear it Out – Make it Do – Or Do Without!

Now my friend is a highly accomplished surgeon who can afford to be at least a little bit frivolous, maybe even careless with his funds, but he is not. He is generous, strategic, and a great steward of all that God has given. He understands that God is the owner, and he simply manages the blessings.

Jesus' question comes after a story He tells about a property manager who had lost his job, and we are invited to reflect on the importance of faithfulness in our everyday lives and the impact that our stewardship has on our spiritual journey (see Luke 16:1-15). In this passage, Jesus emphasizes the necessity of being trustworthy with material possessions. He indicates that how we manage our resources – whether money, time, or talents – reflects our character and readiness for greater responsibilities in the Kingdom of God. It's a profound reminder that even the small, everyday choices we make are significant in the eyes of God.

You've heard the expression, "Don't sweat the small stuff," but Jesus would disagree. Being faithful in little things may seem mundane or unimportant, but it lays the groundwork for greater opportunities. Jesus calls us to recognize that our attitude toward worldly wealth can affect our spiritual depth and influence. If we are careless or untrustworthy with what is temporary, it raises questions about our ability to handle what is eternal.

Jesus challenges us to consider the idea of "true riches." What does it mean to be entrusted with true riches? It suggests that spiritual blessings, such as love, joy, peace, and the fruit of the Spirit, are far more valuable than material wealth. When we remain faithful in the little things, we open ourselves up to experiencing these true riches in abundance.

TREASURE UP: When was the last time I took a look at how I am investing my resources (treasure, talent, and time)? Would it reveal a report that brings honor to my Heavenly Father, or do I need to make some corrections?

Stewardship check-ups like annual physicals are important. Are we intentional about how we use our resources? Do we view them as gifts from God that should be managed wisely? By cultivating a spirit of gratitude and responsibility, we can honor God in all aspects of our lives. Let's ask God to help us be faithful stewards of all He has entrusted to us. May our faithfulness in the small things lead us to greater blessings in our spiritual lives, allowing us to reflect His love and generosity to those around us.

Reading for Reflection: Haggai 1:5-9; 1 Corinthians 4:1-5

I place no value on anything I have or may possess,
except in relation to the kingdom of God. If anything will
advance the interests of the kingdom, it shall be given away
or kept, only as by giving or keeping it I shall most promote
the glory of Him to whom I owe all my hopes in time or eternity.
David Livingstone

◇◇◇

POWER SURGE

Do you think I cannot call on my Father,
and He will at once put at my disposal
more than twelve legions of angels?

Matthew 26:53

My oldest granddaughter loves for me to tell her police stories, anecdotes from a long time ago when I was patrolling the streets of Houston from 11:00 pm to 7:00 am. Her very favorite story involves the arrest of a man we refer to as "Bobby." The truth is I don't remember his name, but I've never forgotten the encounter. Bobby ran a red light right in front of us, not his best decision. When we turned on our lights and eventually our siren, Bobby ignored us and kept traveling, albeit at a slow speed, still not a good decision. Eventually, we got Bobby to pull over after our low-speed chase, and when he got out of the car, I discovered he was one of the largest men I had ever seen. While the story is too long to tell, arresting him was an enormous challenge as he had too much to drink, and he didn't want to be handcuffed. To convince him to cooperate (which was unsuccessful), I reminded him that he might be able to win a fight with my partner (he could have) and me, but we had hundreds of other officers that we could call if needed (and eventually we did).

As Jesus dealt with betrayal and His impending crucifixion, He demonstrated incredible composure and purpose (see Matthew 26:47-56). In fact, He restored the ear of a soldier that had been removed with a sword by one of His disciples. In the face of violence and hostility, He reminded His disciples that He has access to divine resources far beyond human comprehension. The mention of *"twelve legions of angels"* (72,000) signifies an overwhelming force – yet Jesus chooses not to call upon them. Instead, He willingly submits to the path of suffering and sacrifice, fulfilling the prophecy and the redemptive plan for humanity.

Have you considered recently the resources you have at your disposal through faith? Just as Jesus had the power to summon heavenly help, we too, have access to God's strength, wisdom, and grace in our times of need. Yet, like Jesus, we are often called to walk through challenges rather than escape them.

TREASURE UP: What do you need today that will require a miracle? Can you pray specifically in faith, knowing that God has everything you need and is listening to your every prayer?

The choice Jesus made to endure suffering teaches us about the importance of obedience and trust in God's greater purpose. In moments of trial, we may feel the urge to rely solely on our own understanding or seek immediate relief. However, God often calls us to deeper faith and reliance on Him, trusting that He is working all things together for our good. May we seek His strength in our struggles and choose obedience over comfort. In our willingness to follow His path, we can become instruments of His love and grace in a world that desperately needs it.

Let us embrace the power of divine resources and walk boldly in faith, knowing that God is with us every step of the way.

Reading for Reflection: Isaiah 40:28-31; Ephesians 3:20

The greatest story ever told is of a God who so loved the world that He chose to suffer for it.
K.J. Ramsey

◇◇◇

About the Author

Dr. Keith Newman was elected as the fifteenth President of Southern Nazarene University in March, 2017. Before his election, he served Indiana Wesleyan University as Chancellor for IWU-Marion. He previously served as the Vice President for University Relations at Mount Vernon Nazarene University in Mount Vernon, Ohio and for seventeen years in pastoral ministry, including lead pastorates in Van Buren, Arkansas, Houston, Texas and San Diego, California.

Before entering pastoral ministry, he served nine years with the Houston Police Department. During his law enforcement career, he was an Officer in the Radio Patrol and Juvenile Divisions and a Sergeant in the Homicide Division.

Dr. Newman graduated from Houston Baptist University (now Houston Christian University) with a Bachelor of Arts degree, double majoring in History and Christianity, and earned a Master of Ministry from Southern Nazarene University. His Doctorate of Education is from Spalding University with a concentration in Leadership. Dr. Newman's dissertation was an identification and examination of the leadership qualities and characteristics of Dr. J.B. Chapman, an evangelist, pastor, college president, denominational magazine editor, and General Superintendent in the Church of the Nazarene. Dr. Chapman was President of Arkansas Holiness College and Peniel University, contributing institutions to what is now Southern Nazarene University.

Keith met his wife, Carolyn, at the Houston Police Department, where she was also a Sergeant assigned to the Homicide Division. After Carolyn typed a school paper for Keith when he got tied up on a case, and his subsequent dinner invitation began their courtship. Their second date was to a middle school youth group event where Keith was serving as a volunteer youth pastor. Married for 43 years, they have two children: Andy and Alana. Andy is an environmental biologist and he and his wife reside in Houston, Texas. Alana works for an education consulting firm and she and her husband live in Lakeway, Texas. Alana is a 2014 graduate of Southern Nazarene University. Keith and Carolyn have two granddaughters, Avery and Baylin. They call Keith and Carolyn "Pop and GiGi," which have become their favorite titles!

Dr. Newman loves to read stories, hear stories, and tell stories, and he believes God is in the middle of all our stories. In 2018, his first book, LiveLast, was published. Filled with lots of stories, it is based on Jesus' words in Mark 9:35 and calls readers to a "putting others first" lifestyle. His second book, Call Home, a devotional study of the Lord's Prayer, was published in 2023.

With all the opportunities and responsibilities of serving as a university president, spending time with students is at the top of his list of favorite moments each week.

◇◇◇

Notes

Notes

Notes

_____
_____
_____
_____
_____
_____
_____
_____
_____
_____
_____
_____
_____
_____
_____
_____
_____
_____
_____

Notes

Notes

Notes

Notes

Notes

_____

_____

_____

_____

_____

_____

_____

_____

_____

_____

_____

_____

_____

_____

_____

_____

_____

_____

_____

Notes

Notes

www.ingramcontent.com/pod-product-compliance
Lightning Source LLC
LaVergne TN
LVHW051228080426
835513LV00016B/1471